BORN TO FARM IN DEVON

By Horse and Hand-tool at Thurlestone, 1918–1939.

by
Hubert N. Snowdon

© Hubert N. Snowdon

First published Hubert N. Snowdon 1996
Republished by Orchard Publications 1998

2 Orchard Close, Chudleigh, Newton Abbot, Devon TQ13 0LR
Telephone: (01626) 852714

ISBN 1 898964 327

Printed for Orchard Publications by
HEDGEROW PRINT
The Old Creamery, Lapford, Devon EX17 6AE

The Old Harvest.

To save the harvest of old by hand and horse
Was to chance the weather, for good or for worse.
Those labourers, thanking God for daily bread
Now lie at rest with the peaceful dead.

HNS

Contents

Page

PREFACE

To a boy born on a farm in fertile South Devon and to grow up in that closeness to nature pre-destines that he will follow on in that tradition.

A near self-supporting system of mixed farming had evolved over centuries to suit the soil and climate of the area. Because of that a regional sub-culture developed slightly variant to general British agriculture. By comparative speed of change now it advanced little from Iron age and Saxon times and was powered by horses, men and women with simple tools. Yet it was sustainable and helped feed a nation.

The unbelievable changes of this century have overwhelmed it within the lifetime of the author, who was brought up in that old tradition and determined to farm the good earth in the area he loves. Now near eighty years old, and with so many requests to write of that life, he feels obligated to do so.

Trained to physical work, not writing, any of his doubts were dispelled by a letter from a London niece. She, adopted by his sister, was helped by another spinster sister of his who lived with them. Now adult, she wrote to advise that the two sisters were nearing their end. More surprising, remembered as only visiting Thurlestone once at the age of ten, she added how her mum and aunt had so impressed on her their "wonderful upbringing in a lovely place." Also in her own words, "I hope you have good memories of those important years ......I took Mum to see West Buckland just one more time in May. Though she was very ill she was entirely happy that day." The second sister before dying requested to be buried at Thurlestone, stating: "I want to go home."

These sentiments would not have been known except for the niece's writing, and convinces him that there is a place worth writing about if it can be conveyed.

Chapter 1.
The Snowdons in Thurlestone

William and his wife Elizabeth Snowdon lived in the rural parish of Thurlestone in the house facing the village at Rockhill on the Buckland corner. In an 1850s Directory he was listed as fodder merchant; also he was a haulier with horses and farmed some fields. They were my grandparents and their only child Francis William, to become my father, was born there.

They acquired the tenancy of Higher Clanacombe Farm, now known as Cross Parks Farm, and prospered there as good farmers. In 1908 Francis William married Marion Emma Moore, daughter of Roger Moore, a builder at Rose Cottage, West Buckland. They started married life as tenants at Pond Farm, Aveton Gifford and produced three daughters before moving again to Lipton Farm, East Allington. They farmed there through the first Great War and it was where I, Hubert Norman Snowdon, was born on the 11th April 1918. Fifteen months later twin girls completed their family of six.

In 1919 Langman's Farm, West Buckland, Thurlestone, became vacant and as well known Thurlestonians they were given the tenancy, so came "back home" as it were.

Roger Moore my maternal grandfather and family were still at Rose Cottage next door to Langmans, and William Snowdon my other grandfather was still at Higher Clanacombe. He retired in 1920 and moved down to Belle View, West Buckland, just

Buckland, near Thurlestone
Left to right: Belle View 1 & 2. Buckland Cottage, Brook Cottage.
Cider cellar. Langmans Farmhouse. Barn and stable, cow shed & loft
over. Rose Cottage.

1

west of Langmans. Belle View was two brick houses built by Roger Moore, (my maternal grandfather) and later the other house was occupied by a sailor Will Snowdon, my father's cousin. Grandfather Snowdon's two widowed sisters lived in cottages in West Buckland village, and later so did Will's brother George. So we were very much a family group together.

Arrival at Langmans.

Too young, I do not remember the move to Langmans, so relate what I was told. Somehow the livestock was walked, goods and chattels waggoned. My parents drove there in the market trap with me sat on the seat between them, and behind us the baby twins laid end to end in a long drawer. The three older sisters followed on the top of a loaded waggon driven by our horseman to be and one other. They were probably in the charge of Mabel, a Torcross girl, mother's help and my nurse while the twins were young. The horses Madam, Damsel, Nancy and possibly Punch would have made up the two other horse teams.

Imagine now if you can and dare to their feelings, after driving the ten miles by pony trap on a hot and dusty September afternoon, on their first view of "home" after many years absent. They would have come down the ridge road towards Thurlestone and stopped at Clanacombe Head, where the W. Buckland and Bantham road turned off to drop down into the valley. They could look down it to Buckland, on to Bantham, the sea, and Burgh Island in Bigbury Bay. They had seen this beautiful view many times before. But their thoughts and eyes would be on the Langmans' House and the fields opposite, and on Rose Cottage, my mother's and her parents' home next door to Langmans. Then their eyes would have turned right where across one field on the hill stood, white and prominent, Higher Clanacombe Farm house, Frank's past home and where his parents still lived. But they would not have been there because they were at Langmans preparing to help in the arrivals.

Frank would have jumped down from the trap and led the tired and sweating pony down the steep hill to ease the load as it shuffled through the loose stones. No tarmac roads then. Finally, trotting along the valley bottom to arrive in style.

Langmans House.

The house was a large long-house type with seven bedrooms and built into the bank of the steep valley side, facing south. In the centre was a large flagstoned kitchen with a hall either side, each with a stairway to the floor above and a door into the front garden. The west one was front door, and the east back. My older sisters spent their initiation running a circle up one stairway and down the other. The adults of course were very busy. Nine of us to eat and sleep that night.

Off the hall at the west end was a large room that became sitting or dining room as required. Next to the east hall, two steps down from the kitchen, was a cosier sitting room and for a time became children's room. Beyond that was a sunken cellar with a loft over that had access from the farm yard. Above that was a third floor with two bedrooms.

2

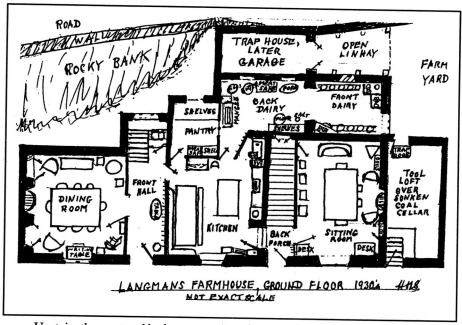

LANGMANS FARMHOUSE, GROUND FLOOR 1930's
NOT EXACT SCALE

Upstairs the west end bedroom was large and known as the best. Next over the hall was a narrower but very good double room. Over the kitchen was a wonderful room, the largest and three-bedded. Over the lower sitting room was our parents' room. A passage behind it led to the two bedrooms over the cellar, one through the other. If four doors were left open one could see end to end of the house. At the rear of the house over the dairy was a back bedroom and over the pantry a bathroom. There were double beds in every room. I have slept in all but the west end one.

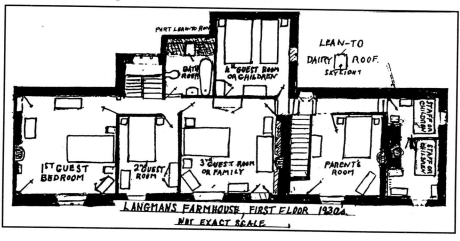

LANGMANS FARMHOUSE FIRST FLOOR 1930's
NOT EXACT SCALE

3

Behind the house above a bank and high wall was the village road, at roof level, with an entrance into the farmyard at the east end and a front gate at the west end, which led down a steep drive to four steps into the front garden. Beside the drive was a shrubbery, which partially hid a cider cellar covered in Virginia creeper. Between that and the house was a thatched summer house.

Langmans Outlook.

The outlook from Langmans across the valley facing the warm south was to say the least picturesque. Running along the length of the house was a front garden, a path, and between that and the house narrow flower-borders. Across the path was lawn 4-5 yards wide and this cut in half by a cobbled path to a rose arch through a low wall which extended the whole length of the front. We sat on this wall a lot, but on the south side it dropped eight feet into a sunken walled garden well stocked with fruit and vegetables. So our front garden was virtually a terrace. Access to the lower garden was down steps through the rose arch. It sloped down to the bottom wall over which were orchards, in turn sloping down to the stream in the bottom of the valley.

Across the stream was a willow plot and rising into the opposite valley side was a vale field scooped out of the hills that rise to the ridge and the sky. Near the centre of that vale field rises a spring, over which spreads a large willow tree. At the bottom corner of the field the thatched roof of a cottage peeps above the prolific bushes in our sheltered sub-tropical valley. Over the ridge on the horizon was a chink of the roof of the first house into Thurlestone. Those were the only buildings in our view and most of the land part of our farm. This was the playground for an idyllic childhood when allowed the freedom and gradually as part of our work place as we grew older.

If I didn't remember that first September arriving at Langmans, I do many others, masses of Michaelmas daisy and golden rod buzzing with bees and insects in the warm sun. Pink and white roses still flowering against the house and colourful drying flowers in the parched borders. Orchards of apples, laden branches hanging over the garden wall. Hedges prolific with wild fruit and berries. Yet in the middle of the village our frontage was not overlooked. Once again we were isolated and continued to be a law unto ourselves, as at Lipton.

Of course callers came to either door of the house. "Intruders" had to come either down the front drive or via the heavy door from the farmyard. We knew the sounds of approachers. Usually they were business, social or workers.

The workers were hard, tough men dressed in corduroy trousers and waistcoat, always with a watch chain across it, striped uncollared white cotton shirts, peak caps, hob nail boots, and leather leggings, but especially in summer without leggings and "Yorks" up, that is leather straps tied under the knees which kept sweaty trouser legs up from dragging over the knees. To work in sweat all day wouldn't be understood to-day. They had hard rough hands, often chapped in winter, and weather hardened ruddy faces, many with pitted ears caused by scratching at chilblains, through working alternately in freezing winds and spring sunshine. They itched unbearably.

These capable men were skilled in a variety of jobs by hand, hedging, walling, ditching, hoeing, harvesting, some worked with horses, whatever was seasonal. Some were particular and, say, wouldn't milk cows or shear sheep.

After wars change is inevitable, but the old mixed farming system persisted after 1918, with dairy herds, beef, sheep, corn and other arable crops, not forgetting cider orchards. All were hand worked or horse powered still. Steam-engines hauled and threshed but now, steam lorries called occasionally to deliver coal and collect grain. Otherwise the common two horses and a waggon delivered and collected one and a half ton loads at a time.

Our mill in the valley was finished working. My father helped there as a boy. It became a butcher's shop with slaughter house. They kept horses for their meat delivery vans and owned steep fields where they grew oats for feed.

Other commodities delivered by horse van were bread, groceries, ironmongery, pots, pans and lamp paraffin, imported fruit and home made ice cream. Packmen walked selling cloth, haberdashery, and all kinds of small goods carried on their backs.

The West Buckland village itself had lost, besides the mill, malt houses converted to dwellings by my grandfather Moore, but had a bakery, a carpenter who made coffins, a builder, a blacksmith, a cobbler, carrier, shop, post office, a chapel, market garden and cider press. Dairy produce was fetched from farms. All that to serve 40 odd houses and, I emphasise, it was near self-sufficient.

In 1919 the aftermath of war was very evident in a quietened, shocked nation trying to come to terms with the terrible loss of its menfolk, and many of those returned

F.W. Snowdon as working master

In market garb with his two dogs

badly maimed. Even we young children were made aware of the fact. I recall that saddened feeling abroad everywhere, worse than in the second war. By shortages austerity ruled, the material payment as well as loss of life. I still possess my old ration book.

We small children were not allowed in the road unaccompanied. Latches were put high on the gates. When taken out for walks, and not fully understanding, we laughed at the funny men we met. They were the wounded, so many, one-legged, one-armed, blind, one-eyed, wheel chaired, shell-shocked. We were sharply reprimanded. Later in Kingsbridge streets I saw these forgotten men sat on the pavements begging.

Regarding the farming start at Langmans, I do not know how much stock was brought with us. Of horses, Madam and Damsel were with us at least to 1920, but according to a diary were now not breeding, and sold. Violet the driving mare was replaced by a grey, Tony. Whitefoot, a very expensive Shire was bought. He ran a nail in his foot and died of blood poisoning. He was insured. Two working mares we had were Nancy, a very sound and willing bay, "not a vice in her!" a loved dealers phrase. She always had a twinkle in her eye. And Blossom, smaller, sturdy, ginger, a little hot but game. Both were good in shafts. Punch was a tall, slight vanner type, a good fore-horse. There was a Dartmoor pony Jessie bought for us children.

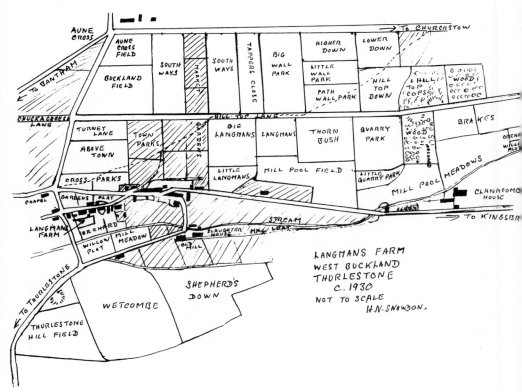

LANGMANS FARM
WEST BUCKLAND
THURLESTONE
c. 1930
NOT TO SCALE
H.N. SNOWDON.

Chapter 2.
Langmans Land and Farm Buildings.

The main block of Langmans land lays behind the house on the south-facing slope of the valley. It is more or less a large square rising steeply at first and gradually less so to the ridge of the hill where a few fields are near level.

This block was our main arable area with fields averaging about four acres. The soil is a light loam friable and easy working, fertile and grateful if the humus content is maintained.

It is more a barley and sheep than dairy farm, because there were no pasture meadows except Wetcombe and Mill Pool meadows which ran as a tongue up the valley from the east end. Also some fields, too steep to plough normally, were grazed. But there are records of these being ploughed, like Shepherds Down and Thurlestone Hill field.

The problems that made Langmans hardworking were first that the farmstead was at one corner of the square which doubles the distance travelled to fields and back than if centrally placed. Second, access to the fields mostly by hard road necessitated climbing the long steep hill to Aune Cross and along the ridge road. There was access along the valley road and up through steep fields to the better arable fields when dry, but near impossible when wet. That meant the long trip via Aune Cross and down from the ridge road. Also there was no direct outlet to the fields from the farmyard, and only the valley fields were watered.

The farm buildings were more or less terraced. North of the road was a large threshing barn with the stable and hayloft over at the east end. Opposite at road level was a hayloft with cowshed and calf houses beneath. South of that the farmyard and then a row of pigsties with access from the orchard below them. There were two cart sheds and a granary on stone pillars. Rose Cottage and garden were east of that and east again was

Feeding tame lambs on the bottle

our Caute Court off yard with a threshing barn converted to cattle fattening shed with loft over and another separate small hay loft with open linhey beneath. Also a large lean-to shed against the large barn.

Sickly lambs brought in for warmth and milk were my first encounter with the animals in the kitchen, and Help the sheep dog, he guarded the twins faithfully. Cats! My mother could not resist cats. On the lawn we reared small chickens and ducks in coops. We children watched, through the back bedroom window, when Whitefoot was being buried in the orchard. Among the trees we saw men chop him up with axes and dig the pit.

In the yard I would have seen the horses and cows come and go. Mabel helped to milk, turn the cream separator, and feed the calves and pigs with the separated milk. Some milk was scalded on pans and the skim milk was also fed. Surplus cream as usual made butter. The girls helped, and myself, when old enough.

The barn yard poultry were fed with grain twice daily, and eggs collected evenings. Some stole nests in all kinds of hidden places, needing periodic searches, the cause of stale and proverbial "bad eggs" turning up to customers. Unfound nests were hatched by the broody culprit, which came home with a brood.

Jessie, our pony, was quiet, obedient, and absolutely passive to any treatment we six and visiting children could mete out to her.

Through the war the government bought grain, barley reached £21 per ton. By continuous corn cropping farms became played out. Langmans was full of such stubbles. Then the Corn Laws were repealed in 1921. Barley price down to £4½ per ton. How's that for a wage cut? My father went to arbitration because of the poor state of his fields and got the rent reduced. Rents were about £1 per acre at the time.

My grandfather William Snowdon retired from Clanacombe Farm in 1920 and came down to live near us in West Buckland. One of my earliest memories is at Clanacombe Farm, on the top of the stairs, bare to the wood, when they were clearing out I suspect. Someone said: "Mind you don't fall!" Down I went to the bottom and knocked out my two front teeth.

In 1922 we were requested to start a milk round in the village. Previously milk was fetched at a third approach to our house through the farm yard to the dairy window, where customers could ring a bell through to the kitchen for their requirements. Milk was 3d. a pint, cream and butter (seasonal) 1s to 2s per pound, eggs 6d to 1/9d per dozen.

At first, on the round, the milk was carried in hand churns and dipped out into customers' jugs. Then when requested to serve Clanacombe and Bantham Jessie was put into the governess cart with a larger churn on the seat and my oldest sister, still at school, was sent off. In the event of her not finishing in time for school my father would meet her and finish.

Also in 1922 a new cattle market was opened just on the edge of Kingsbridge, at Ropewalk, known still as Dodbroke market, because there were two towns divided by a creek. Infill has made them one, but in name Dodbroke market remained and Kingsbridge

Pony Jessie and governess cart ready for milk round

had an annual fair, both held in the street. I have attended both as a toddler. Sheep and pigs were penned in with hurdles, but horses and cattle, often loose, were hustled in place by the farmers. I, bustled around trying to keep in touch with parents, and small, anything I could see was through men's legs. That way face to face with a long-horned cow that I didn't know, head low, salivating off the tongue and bellowing for its weaned calf, was a bit frightening when under four years.

But I was four years of age when at home I asked to milk. Mabel took me into the shed with the easiest cow, but I couldn't manage.

With our farm being in the village and the sheep on the hill in fields, seldom were they at the farm so I didn't see them closely. One day there was a ewe and lamb in a shed behind a hurdle for some reason. Curious, I approached and looked through the hurdle. The ewe stared me back with bland brown unseeing eyes and its head level with mine, which it tossed, snorted and stamped its foot at the same time. I retreated, deciding that I did not like sheep, a little afraid.

Father, wishing to initiate me to the farm, asked would I like to walk round the farm with him? I hesitated, then said: "I will if you don't go to see the sheep." Of course, that was partly the purpose of his walk. But when there I wouldn't go in the field despite his encouragement. He gathered them to the gate. I stood outside shivering with fear.

Soon we had orphan lambs brought home to the kitchen to be reared on the bottle. First my sisters and then me were given our own lambs to rear, and growing up with them soon overcame any fears.

Chapter 3
The Kitchen, Dairy and Wash House

The kitchen had a long elm dining table against the west wall and was well lit by the window in the south wall. There was a bench fixed from the window round the wall as far as the end of the table. Over the bench was a high shelf where home made jam was stored. On the kitchen side of the table was a long form.

On the east wall was a large open hearth with a copper on the right side for scalding pans of cream. Next to it was the main door down two steps to the back door. Behind the door in the west wall was the sink and draining board. To the left of the hearth was a large cooking range, coal-burning, and responsible for our cooked meals. On the north wall in the centre was a large 'hold all' dresser. To the west side was a door into the pantry, and on the east side a door into the double dairy. Between that and the dresser stood a windsor chair where father laced and unlaced his hob-nail boots - the only chair. In the middle of the kitchen was a fairly large sturdy pine work table.

Father was up by 6 a.m., if not earlier, lit faggot sticks in the hearth and hung the kettle on the chimney crook. While that boiled he laced up his boots and went into the dairy with two slices of bread and plastered them over with cream to eat with his cup of tea. Then he went out to the men and the cows.

If anyone got up with him they could have cream too - a way of getting us up. Then the women came down, lit the range and prepared breakfast before 8 a.m. in those early days. Often fried eggs, fat bacon and potatoes or bread, sometimes cold boiled pork, jam

or marmalade. We children were favoured with cream and porridge after the men had left again.

There would be yesterday's pans of milk to scald on the stove, or, if many, the copper would also be lit. The previous day's surplus milk would be stood in pans in the dairy to rise the cream. Skim milk for the calves would be warmed to blood heat. Then the washing up of breakfast dishes and dairy utensils. They were sterilized in boiling water.

The Dairy.

The dairy as usual on farms was along the north-east part of the house, the coolest. Entry from the kitchen was first into the back dairy, which held a flour barrel, salting pans for pork, pickled butter, preserved eggs, a large meat safe, a clothes mangle, hangings for wet weather and working clothes. Behind the door were brushes and brooms. There were shelves for pots of this and tins of that, and things in everyday use.

The front dairy was light and airy by perforated zinc windows. Here only milk, cream, butter and eggs were kept and the end window into the yard opened as our shop window. There was a bell pull outside which rang through to the kitchen. The enamel pans of milk and cream were held on pine forms, known as 'mares'. They stood along both side walls. In the corner by the shop window was a pine table which held the butter scales and weights, a tin for the cash, and a cash diary. A dish held the milk measures and cream spoons and skimmers. Half pound and pound butter pats, wrapped in greaseproof paper were kept on the slate window shelves. The eggs were in a large basket on a three-corner shelf.

CREAM PANS AND MILK PAILS AIRING OUTSIDE WASH HOUSE

11

The walls and ceilings were regularly whitewashed for freshness, and the floors, like the kitchen blue slate flagstones, were scrubbed often. They were well worn and uneven through use.

In the kitchen the ceiling was wooden raftered and stained by years of smoke from fires and oil lamps to a blackened mahogany colour. There were various crooks screwed up to it. We just used some to hang empty baskets. There was also a gun rack which supported two twelve-bore shot guns. There was a short curtain hung to hide the long shelf of two-pound jars of home made jam. Below that two round tin pictures, copies of Constable, and between them a framed picture of frolicking horses and foals.

Working Day in the Kitchen.

After breakfast for the outside workers, lunch prepared in the kitchen, was carried out by them to their place of work that day. It was eaten at 10 a.m. in the 20 minutes allowed. Incidentally, Council road workers and some others lunched at 9.30 a.m. The usual lunch was bread and cheese, or fat pork and bread, with or without pickled onion, and was washed down from the daily 3 pints allowance of cider or cold tea. Any village boy who came looking for work was given breakfast. Then we knew he had one good meal to work on.

In the centre of activity, the busy kitchen, butter was made by hand from the surplus scalded cream two or three times a week. Always, there was preparation for the main meal of the day, dinner, eaten at 12.30 p.m. Especially busy were roasting days, cooking for ten or more, a meat joint and fresh home-grown vegetables; sometimes delicious stews, and all followed with boiled fruit puddings or tarts with cream. The diet would be considered fattening to-day, but necessary with our output of energy working with horses and hand tools. Seldom was seen a fat belly among farm workers.

After dinner while the stove was still hot, and I've seen the top plate glowing red when in full use, tins of cakes and buns were baked, and perhaps something slow-cooking for supper.

Unless there were special things to do afternoons, when all was clear, the red-faced ladies retired upstairs for a well-earned rest and 'tidy up themselves'. Never quite admitting it, to be idle was thought near criminal. After 4 p.m. it started again from all directions: children came in from school, the workers who milked from the fields, and the women came downstairs to make the cherished cup of tea for all before milking and the evening yard work began. Feeding, bedding, watering of cows, horses, calves, pigs and chickens; milk to be turned through the cream separator, eggs to collect. The hired men finished at 5.30 p.m., the household staff hopefully for supper at six p.m., another main meal.

That meal could be more high-tea style, something lightly cooked, fresh local fish, a fry-up, or cold meat with salad, or something on toast, followed by a sweet, fruit salad, jelly, stewed fruit, junket, apple tart - a popular standby - all with custard or cream.

Diverting from food momentarily, and to find that hub of the household silent is unbelievable, but to walk into that kitchen first, after 4 p.m., the silence was almost eerie.

After school I did this often, and now recall the simple soft sounds that would break that silence: the kettle for tea on the stove start singing, the closed down fire below crack, the cat on the cushion in the chair begin purring, the slow tick-tock, tick-tock of the clock.

But, being a boy I made quickly to the cupboard and took two currant rock buns from their tin, before the women appeared and would hand me just one. Later when bolder and older I crept into the dairy and spooned cream on top. Tricky, because the latch on the dairy door clicked loudly - deft handling needed. Cream and fat pork, we thrived on it! Luxury, unhealthy, expensive to-day, then cheaply home-produced, except for the sweat of our brows, and they renewed our energy output. "Plain Fare", my father named it, and it was, compared with profit-motivated adulterated food now. Bought luxury food was a rarity.

After supper in summer we were outside again. In winter we resorted to one sitting room or other with a log fire. We alternated rooms to air them from damp. Seldom were evenings idle: sewing, darning, writing, accounts. We children played table games after homework. Our light was a table oil-lamp. Finally there would be milk or cocoa sops by candlelight. The candle-sticks and matches were kept on a high shelf over the kitchen door. With lamp and fire extinguished they were left to cool for the morning chore of clearing ashes, cleaning and refilling the oil lamps.

The Wash House.

The weekly wash had to be witnessed to be believed and was such an ordeal for the womenfolk. It was general in the 1920s with no washing machines or collecting

LANGMANS WASH HOUSE

laundry vans in the country, and mechanical aids available were expensive, thought only for the wealthy.

Wash houses were often separate from the house and some just a galvanised iron shed with a copper in the corner and fire under to heat water. Our wash house was large, about square, and built at the lower end of the garden against the yard and orchard wall, of galvanised iron with the roof under-boarded to stop steam condensing and dripping water. Nearly central over a well was a pump and a large granite trough emptying into a sink. The water was very hard. Outside was a rainwater butt collecting off the main house roof. That water was soft, and preferred if available. Inside on the north side was a shelf of small tools and the cream separator in daily use. By the trough was a wooden form where milk buckets and utensils were washed.

On washdays the copper in the lower corner of the east wall was lit at 6 a.m. to boil water by the time a washerwoman arrived. Two wooden rectangular washtubs on rails along the rest of the east wall, contained the clothes, preferably put in suds to soak the night before. An oval tin bath on the wooden form was also used. I am not familiar with the washing process, but the clothes were rubbed and scrubbed by hand with the aid of soap, soda, a little paraffin and a blue bag to whiten, then put in the copper to boil. Finally, hardly visible through steam and smoke, the clothes were wrung by hand, put into the large wicker basket and carried down the steps to the walled garden, and hung on wire lines to dry which stretched the length of the paths.

The washing for nine, from sheets to socks and coarse farm wear, was a full day's work for at least two. A washer woman, M. and my mother shared the load between dairy

RAINWATER BUTT AND YARD DOOR

work and cooking. Many a Monday I came home from school to see them exhausted and red-eyed, just clearing up. They were very short-tongued if I selfishly asked for something unnecessary, except Mrs F. She was always cheerful, a wonderful worker, washing for many in the village, a wonderful character. She also darned our socks.

Chapter 4.
Early Childhood.

When very young the twins and I slept in the back bedroom overlooking the yard - the twins in the double bed and I in the single, noted for rocking myself to sleep. On wet days we romped about the beds until called, often quite late. Washed and breakfasted we then sat or were put on the top ledge of the kitchen window seat with our feet on the wider bottom one. This happened to be very convenient for the adults to put on our socks, then boots, and lace them up. This is where we learned to tie our first bows. Also higher from the floor than our normal height, we often sat to see more of what was going on. Comfortable there, we spent hours happily, especially on wet days. Children love to be near to and to watch adults. We were allowed to and did romp in the lower sitting room, but it soon came to squabbles and someone would run crying to the kitchen.

When dry and sunny we played for hours especially in the summer house and in the garden, not allowed beyond. Even on frosty mornings we were sent out well wrapped up and when the sun appeared it was always warm in that sheltered southern front.

In 1922 I wanted to go to school with my three older sisters, so I climbed the hill to Thurlestone C. of E. school a week before my fourth birthday.

At school, too young, I found it strange and didn't want to sit where asked. I kicked up, upsetting the whole room. At last in an attempt to quieten me they produced a box of building bricks, beautiful geometric shapes and colours. That was a mistake, as

they would find out. The bricks appealed to my artistic nature more than they realised. We never had toys so bright and beautiful, always plain and second hand. I built castles and bridges to my heart's delight. Next day they took them away. I threw a tantrum the likes of which they wouldn't want too often. I was in the senior room with my three sisters and two teachers. None could pacify me. I remember a second cousin, a girl ten years older trying: "You came to school to learn, not to play." Subdued in the end and pride very hurt, I was to learn that you didn't get your own way in school.

Childhood with Ringworms.

So I was escorted to the junior room to the only empty seat, beside a boy no-one else would sit with because he had a huge ring worm on his forehead the size of a teacup. In a week or two I had caught them in my hair and they spread all over my head. I gave them to my twin sisters and for two and a half years I was home from school before we were rid of them. My three older sisters were sent next door, with their aunt, and not allowed near us. Three little kiddies in isolation, painfully scrubbed daily with strong solution, we cried, otherwise played. We wore little home-made skull caps to hide our shame with all hair shaved off, and to stop germs spreading hopefully.

Our ringworms persisted. There was talk for us to be X-rayed, the new wonder, to what point I never understood. There was talk that our hair would never grow again if we did. Our mother and Mabel persevered relentlessly, as always, with ointments and scrubbings. Eventually it cleared, and our hair grew again. To-day I suspect ringworm could be halted promptly.

Snowdon family with dog Shep, 1924.
Note - twins' hair just growing after ringworm.

17

Sometimes we were given a sweet, an apple, or a peeled orange to appease us. With the orange I was told to share it out. At that time I had no conception of thirds, only of halves. So I split the orange in half, and one half again, and gave my sisters one quarter each and kept the other half for myself. I knew that I was having more than they, and felt guilty about it, but at that age couldn't see differently. They never complained.

We had few outdoor toys so made our fun, mixed soil in water and made mudpies in the shape of loaves, let them dry in the sun and delivered them round the garden in all kinds of cricks and crannies as a baker's round. We added pebbles as eggs when a load of beach pebbles from Thurlestone as replacement was tipped down our drive - beautiful rounded stones, all sizes and colours. We made mini-farms and gardens with any available materials, which kept us absorbed for hours.

We did not like to be photographed in our skull caps. If there were any taken they are probably destroyed. Playing our delivery rounds we would have taken trips "up the lane" as we called it. Between the cider cellar and the north wall of the walled garden was a narrow lane at the end of which was a large three seater lavatory, two holes for mums and dads and lower smaller one for children. It was well built, off the corner of the garden, of stone with an interesting slate roof, because they were very small slates, except those round the roof edges, no bigger than tea plates, and every one pegged with wooden pegs. Very old, I would think sherds left over from the original farmhouse slates. The whole building was grown over with "old man's beard" (wild clematis). We entered under a tunnel of it, which had to be cut back after it grew so fast. There was a little square window overlooking the walled garden, with a pleasant view outside. I often watched small birds and goings-on in the garden from that hidey-hole.

LANGHANS 3 SEAT LAVATORY 'UP THE LANE'

The old fashioned three-seater outdoor lavatory "up the lane" at the end of the garden was used regularly by staff and household when they were outside with farm or garden muddied boots. Then we were not allowed to use the inside one upstairs.

I soon learned to climb the front gate and undo the top latches. One day a message came to the farm: "Hubert and the twins are playing in the mill stream at Clanacombe, three-quarters of a mile away."

We were forbidden to enter the big threshing barn because of dangerous machines and tools there. Up eight steps were two big half doors one above the other. I had learned to climb over the bottom when the top was open, wishing to see what we were forbidden. At first vision of these machines and things I was fascinated. One day I dragged my twin sisters over the door, the second one slid the calf of her leg down a hay knife with a blade two foot long. She carries the scar to-day. When in other barns we often fell down the hay racks, difficult to see when stuffed with hay for the cattle. Sometimes we fell under the horses, and luckily were never stepped on. Somehow animals often tolerate children. Once I saw a toddler take away a bone from a big sheep dog of ours that I would have thought twice about attempting. He gave it up quite willingly, as if pleased to oblige her.

Early Christmases.

Austerity prevailed after the First World War, and a double dose more so normally, as both sides of our family were nearly puritanical. But at Christmas, the main festival of Christians, it was well celebrated in Victorian style, with plenty of food and greenery decoration, much of it home-grown. Relatives came to us, because we were tied to the farm, and enjoyed the farm fare and atmosphere. They brought their offerings, shop-bought, new and glittering. We children enjoyed that.

Children's stockings were filled with simple gifts, a penny and an orange in the toe, a bar of chocolate, sweets, nuts, mini-toys and puzzles, perhaps a book, and an individual present tied at the top.

Sleepily we heard rustlings in the night, but dare not wake lest Santa didn't stop. Early in the morn we woke to the clamour every family knows. The farm work and milk round were bustled through and we never opened the rest of the presents until everyone was in. Everyone was very redfaced, the outside workers from their hurry, and the cooks from extra breakfasts to fry and already joints and vegetables cooking for the big one at 1 p.m. There were chicken, ducks or goose and always with roast pork, never turkey at that time, thought to be an extravagant luxury of the wealthy. Then traditional pudding with silver 3d. pieces and one sixpence. In the afternoon, some slept, some walked with the children. At 4 p.m. came a cup of tea and Christmas cake. The farming few went out to the yard again to see to the needs of the animals. The cooks prepared the big supper: cold meat and all the trimmings followed by sweetmeats and crackers. In paper hats we played games, mainly for the children's sake until bedtime, and by the silence afterwards the exhausted adults were glad to sit quiet with a cup of tea or perhaps a glass of wine. Alcohol was never over-indulged in or encouraged. Cider was available at meals. Boxing Day was quieter, the men sporting, rabbiting, hunting, perhaps a football match, with a big meal and party in the evening. On one day we always gave the village children a party in our big kitchen. On the Sunday we all attempted to attend the Chapel services.

Quiet Valley.

Like our kitchen, on a calm still afternoon there were times when our valley seemed completely silent and then intermittent simple rural sounds the clearer emphasised it: a single sheep bleat on the hill, a cock crow, a rook call. In Thurlestone hill field, the one west above the vale field Wetcombe, a ploughman quietly speaks to his horses, the plough wheel squeaks across the field. A cow coughs across on Shepherds Down, the hill to the east. The rumble of cart wheels along the road to the old mill. The chink-chink of the blacksmith's hammer, a woodsman chopping, children playing.

None of these sounds were excessive. What could be? The steamroller rumbled and chuff-chuffed, the thresher hummed pleasantly. Dogs barked, a weaned calf and cow called. Once a year Kingsbridge Town band marched playing through the village. Musical, we ran to greet them. Mabel fancied the little drummer boy. Church bells were musical, especially heard coming over the hill and fields from near a mile away.

Our mother always timed our going to chapel, just around the corner, by the church bells. "Come on, the bells are stopped, we'll be late." To know exact time was difficult. Spring clocks and pendulums were unreliable. On a farm with so much to do before going anywhere we were always rushed, seldom early. There were no Big Bens or Radio pips then.

Possibly our greatest sound came each Spring with the dawn chorus. A crescendo of a thousand birds singing their hearts out. The only comparable likeness I know of is Ludwig Coch's rendering of a dawn chorus. I remember mother calling us: "Come on, get up, the sun is shining, can't you hear the birds singing?" Three or four cuckoos among them, not just one.

On still nights, in bed, with a yellow full moon shining through the blue, we could hear wavelets intermittently swishing softly on the pebbles at Thurlestone beach a mile away. How easy to romanticise. Then suddenly a barn owl let out its blood-curdling screech just outside on a barn roof, the spell changed, and one looked for shadows at the window. Tawny owls were more plentiful, seeming more friendly with their slower too-whoos and hoots to one another.

Chapter 5.
1923-7.

In 1923 my grandfather Moore died next door at Rose Cottage. He was a tall, quiet, thinking man, respected and a good builder. He worked hard to maintain the family above water. If caught dozing he always replied that that was his thinking time. Grandmother was the very strict dominant one of her brood of six.

In 1924 I started school again with the twins, now aged five, for the first time, and in the charge of the next oldest sister. The following year she joined the oldest two girls attending a new private school set up in West Buckland by newcomers Mr. and Mrs Sutton, a very intelligent and talented couple. It thrived and later moved to Dartmouth.

We youngsters climbed the hill to Thurlestone Church of England village school daily, ran home for dinner, and climbed the hill back again. Some rough winter days we carried sandwiches and stayed. Occasionally in summer at 4 p.m. we ran down across path fields to Bantham beach where Mabel or someone would meet us for swims, tea, and excited fun among the rocks and dunes in endless sunny days that children remember.

When a bit older father told me I must bring the cows home for milking on the way from school. So I took a direct route across fields to Wetcombe daily, and gathered them back to the farm yard.

Starting school again from our forced sheltered life I not only learned good things, but mixing with all the kids I learned some choice and rude language that really shocked me. In Devon County Council readjustments South Milton were unlucky to lose their Senior school. The pupils were made to walk to Thurlestone school, 1½ miles. They showed their resentment with very bad behaviour. Most of all the boys, Thurlestone too, outside school, reverted to rustic hooliganism. Boys will be boys.

Early Visitors.

At least by 1924 we started taking in paying visitors at Langmans, as farmhouse accommodation was becoming popular. It was found as an alternative to hotels very wholesome, on full board, and cheaper. The first guests seemed to be the genteel, often couples who one or both for health reasons were advised to come, and could afford to do so.

Next door at Rose Cottage my aunt had started with such a couple. Rose Cottage was earlier a farmhouse, known as Caute House, and with six rooms they were turned to income after our grandparents died there.

We started similarly with requests. Often these were long lets through winter before whole family holidays became common.

Their arrival was by G.W.R. to Kingsbridge, and then to the farm by horse wagonette or the new "motor taxis." From then on without transport of their own, they walked a little for a daily constitutional and for the rest of the day seemed just to sit around. For £1 - £2 per week full board, and waited on hand and foot with fresh farm produce home cooked, from clotted cream to cider, and a wood fire thrown in, they were on a good wicket. Or, I thought so from a very early age, compared to our working lives. Some I doubted, simply because they could afford to be 'delicate,' more hypochondria than real.

One Methodist minister lodged with us all one winter with a genuine nervous breakdown I believe. Knowledgeable, keen on the stars, he took me out on clear nights sorting out the galaxies. He was appalled at my lack of education by his standards and tried very hard to improve me, speaking in his very Lancashire accent. But, my word! Few visitors then or now, especially from cities, have any idea the wealth of knowledge we were accumulating living near nature and from it.

He wrote a book, "The Eternal Purpose." I never read the copy he kindly gave me fully until recently. I'm afraid it would be considered 'old hat' with to-day's advancements. He tried hard.

Farmhouse Repairs.

In 1925 our farmhouse needed a major repair. Two men, a Mr. Cave and Mr. Hutchings, were sent from the landlord's Plymouth timber yard, then in depression, to lodge in our house. Together with his agents in Aveton Gifford, who had building and carpentry businesses, they were to carry out the work. Tall wooden scaffold poles were stuck up vertically round the house in tubs of sand, and two tiers of horizontal boards tied to them with ropes. Then the three chimneys were rebuilt with brick, smart pots on top. The whole roof was reslated with lovely purple Welsh slate. Several rotting windows were replaced which had much larger glass panes than the former ones. Next, the patchy and cracking lime plaster falling off the front wall, helped in the past by tiny fingers I may add, was ripped off and replaced by pebble-dash of lovely Thurlestone beach pebbles drawn down by our own horses and carts.

Bored in the evenings, the two men Cave and Hutchings, acquired a squeeze box, wonderful for us, - no other music much but hymns. Other workers came in, it went well for a time. Then a big fall-out: who owned it? It disappeared, found years after in a heap of brambles, ruined!

We are ten with pony Jessie in 1924

Twins with friend and valley rich with orchard blossom
before many elm trees were cut down in 1925

Some of the young men builders kept asking me to fetch my oldest sister out. She, about fifteen, was growing attractive, and made herself scarce.

The two men stayed on and felled 70 trees in our prolific valley. Most trees remained where they fell, and made wonderful places for us to clamber and swing, also bridges across the stream for years.

1927

In 1927 were three notable events. My father had a hernia operation and was in bed recuperating at home when the second event, a severe blizzard, struck on Christmas eve. We woke to a real white one. Of course, father's concern was for the animals. The cows indoors at night were milked first and helpers carried milk in churns round the village to customers as the pony cart couldn't travel. News came in that the pigs were afloat in their sty from melting snow. The three colts, now weaned, were in the field farthest from the house. The horseman was despatched to check them before the outlying cattle. He reported they were safe in the shelter of the adjoining wood, where the grass was blown clear of snow. They were staring a bit, seeing snow for the first time, their coats were stuck up on end but shining well. A feed of hay would put them right for the day.

The sheep were in Thurlestone hill field opposite the house. Grandfather Snowdon would check them. He set out with father's one-man sheep dog on a rope, hoping Shep would round up the flock for the count. We children watched through the window. Shep was given the order and let off the rope. He put his tail between his legs and ran home.

Grandfather when angry had a roar that would wake the dead.

That year Christmas was had where you were stuck, whether home or not. Roads were filled to hedge tops. Days later an uncle, with us for Christmas, clambered five miles to Kingsbridge and back for bread yeast.

In the third event our village football team won our M.P., Major Harvey's, Challenge Cup. We were football mad before, more so after. Outside the village inn we small boys were offered to drink from the cup - my first taste of beer. I thought it horrid. Two neighbouring farmers and two relatives of mine were in that team. Later there was a celebration dinner in the barn of the team captain, a farmer.

Chapter 6.
Thurlestone Church of England School.

There arrived a new young head teacher from Lancashire, Miss Gill, ginger and smart. Obviously nervous, blushed at the drop of a pin. She was a dedicated teacher and disciplinarian. She correctly lectured us on how bad we were: she cajoled and badgered us to learn.

As a C. of E. school the parson took prayers every morning and complained we did not know our catechism. We were kept in from play until we did.

Daily she made us learn and repeat our mathematical tables up to 12 times table. She retained us out of school hours until we could answer directly any multiplication thrown at us. She caned us on the hands with that deadly weapon the blackboard pointer. The junior mistress also had painfully poked us in the ribs with one when we were not paying attention. On the good side Miss Gill organised outdoor games: netball on the local football pitch, rounders in the school playground. Dividing the school in two, we excitedly battled to win. Inside we learned Country Dancing and school plays, acted near Christmas at the Thurlestone Hotel. Reluctantly she allowed the boys football on the local pitch. We were football mad and played continuously in the playground and outside, Buckland and Bantham against Thurlestone. B. & B. always won.

We liked all that, but Miss Gill continued to rule with the iron (wooden) rod. So much so that one dinner time South Milton boys and those of us who stayed at school called a Council of War and decided to hide the rod. Fortunately, we found the drawer

Thurlestone C. of E. School 1928

unlocked, and stole it and hid it behind one of the large pictures on the wall depicting the Ten Commandments. One day, we having annoyed the caretaker, she threatened to tell teacher. Oh dear! the caretaker knew our secret. Another Council of War. We took the pointer out into the field next door, which was being ploughed, and buried it under the furrow, where I suppose it rotted away. Nothing was ever brought up about it in school.

Despite our opposition , Miss Gill's good teaching was having effect. Unaware by us at the time she was becoming appreciated and respected, especially by the girls. She gave a lot of herself in shaping us.

Education could be completed at the village school to the leaving age of fourteen years. Many did this when there were more farm workers' children at school than now. The big ones bullied me, a farmer's son, because their fathers had to work for the likes of mine. Whatever the sin, as their fathers saw it, was visited upon the sons. The big girls were worse, they didn't disguise their hate when in the mood and the chance occurred. Once they singled me out on a paper chase. We were in front with the hares. Teacher was behind with the hounds. First the verbal abuse, then the thumps - I ended up in the brambles. Some of the same girls got hold of me outside our football field gate. I was on my way to take our cows home, and getting it "a bit thick in the neck." I was never a pugilist, but in self-defence one girl ended up with a gushing bloody nose. After a second attempt with the same result I was left alone, getting bigger and stronger anyway.

A surprise came when Miss Gill announced that I and three others were to sit the entrance scholarship exam to the Grammar School. A bigger surprise followed when we were told we would need to do homework. No more running out to play on the farm after tea.

I was made to sit in the sitting room, alone, with pen, ink and paper. Aged nine, I felt gaoled and sat stunned, never to lose that traumatic feeling. Is this what growing up to be an adult means? I thought, was I to become a despised "pen-pusher"? I had visions of pinched little Dickensian clerks sitting on high stools at high desks in dingy little offices. I had seen them many times in Kingsbridge. They existed, real, in Victorian offices all over the town.

My first prep: Write a short essay on "Is it better to live in the town than the country?" I already had strong views on that. The result: "Do it again tonight." Since in my life I have prayed for that essay to turn up again. It has, twice, and on both I also failed. I still hold the same views, and add, I have never had a country-bred teacher. I have the essays now, accordingly too bad to reproduce despite their rural sentiments. I'm confused: who understands what?

(While writing this, 2/12/94, I've just watched six gold finches in my garden. What jewels they are, and cost nothing!)

Grammar School Entrance Exam.

After nearly a year of homework, at about Easter time I contracted chicken pox followed by whooping cough and was home from school for six weeks. It was decided as a result that none of us should sit the exam, as we would be young enough the following May.

That horrid day arrived, more trauma, to sit scared in the Grammar School main hall at 20 Fore Street, Kingsbridge, a huge drab room, brown, panelled, with high windows, a few dark portraits of the founder and a past head master or two. And, most imposing, a high boxed seat affair like a wide pulpit with a carved wooden canopy over that. It was like a courtroom in which we were to be judged. We sat at desks to answer written questions. The long-faced deputy Headmaster wearing a black cloak down to the ground strode silently round. He was like an evil-eyed raven looking for carrion.

In the afternoon the headmaster sat in a Windsor chair alone in that colourless empty hall and called us in one by one. He, also, was wearing that same depressing black cloak, and smiled: "Come along, don't be shy," - as if that made any difference to my awe.

There was a queer shaped hat, black, on the window shelf. If he had put that on I'm sure I would have received the "death" sentence: "You've failed." His severe look returned, "This is called tots, general questions to see what you know. What happened in 1066?" I was silent. "Or 1588?" I hadn't a clue. "Come on, you've done some history!"

Until that day history to me was a picture book of cave-dwellers, with fire alight cooking, the family wearing skins, and men with hunting spears. It seemed a good simple life. Then the nasty Romans came with Julius Caesar's marching legions carrying swords to conquer them, Good King Arthur burnt some cakes, King Harold lost an eye. There was good Queen Bess and Queen Victoria, of whom we had a bust in our school.

It seemed I could answer very few questions and the pit of my stomach doubted that I wanted Grammar School. Weeks later I learned that I had passed, with a long wait to start in the September term. 1066 and all that, Phew!

Chapter 7.
Horses, 1925-9.

About 1925 the mares Nancy and Blossom produced foals, and Nancy had another the following year. They were my father's pride and joy.

Of Langmans Farm it has been said that it takes a good horse to pull an empty wagon, leave alone a full one, up the long steep hill from Buckland to Aune Cross. We've known horses that couldn't do it. Most of our farm traffic was up and down that hill, making Langmans a hard-working farm.

The hill was narrow with few passing places, bad enough with horse traffic, but, how horsemen hated the arrival of the first motor cars. One day our horseman A. with our mare Nancy, and me sat in the wagon, met a car on the hill. A few yards up the hill behind the car was a passing place. The driver refused to back up. "Look", said A., "I can only hold this mare so long head uphill, and if she starts she'll take you, car and all." The driver backed up.

Nancy's two colts Duke and Prince with Blossom's one, Lion, were broken in about 3 years old. Their sire was an exceedingly powerful and spirited entire. These qualities were passed on. To tame them from their natural fear and wariness the process started at birth by carefully patting and touching them while at their mother's side when the chance occurred. When weaned and in the field on their own, to help gain their trust, a food box was hung on the gate. When passing we put a few oats in it and called to them. Warily they came to food and eventually allowed themselves to be patted and haltered and led round. It needed a deal of patience, but their high spirits were not broken to the obedience needed for their future safe working.

For full breaking they were trotted round on a long rein until completely tired out. This was repeated at intervals until they were so completely exhausted that they could not resist when harness was strapped on them, or even when a man rode on their back. When harness broken, one was hitched between two old mares pulling a harrow round a field. This was to learn the commands and drill of arable work, and finally in shafts for cart work. I saw little of this, and at a distance, too dangerous for small boys to be around.

My father was a superb horseman and by his sheer tenacity in training these spirited young shires he brought them under command to the obedience of his word. Other than those he bred, those he bought were usually sound. Buying is tricky.

About this time old Jessie was changed for Lady, a similar Dartmoor pony. Tony the gray cob was sold to a Kingsbridge grocer for pulling his delivery cart, and visited us regularly on his round. Tony was replaced by Prudence, a good sound bay mare cob, bought from a farm sale at South Milton. She would drive, ride, or work in chains on arable, but alone. She was a very prudent lady and would not work with another horse, nor breed. We relied on her for years for the milk round, marketing, hiring out for riding, and arable work.

At times we rented summer grazing away and put bullocks there for the summer. We walked with them there and back, however far. Occasionally we rode ponies. I had to be introduced to this droving on strange roads and, at the particular time on Jessie, was too young and more nuisance than I was worth. I was not quick enough at cross roads to see what was wanted, nor to get ahead as required. Father became more and more annoyed with me. When I let past some cattle down one road, and the rest another, hurling abuse at me he charged past, like a cowboy, after one lot while sending the dog after the other. Non-plussed, I was stuck fast. Having gathered the cattle somewhere, he galloped back, still very annoyed, to collect me. We were very late, nearly dark, when we closed the gate on the cattle that summer night. We used back lanes to avoid traffic. Turning for home, exhausted and annoyed, he told me to hurry. "I can't keep up, I don't know the way." He galloped on. "The pony will bring you home." It was dark, I was frightened and lost. Then, Jessie's gut having shrunk, the saddle slipped round and I fell off. Luckily I held onto the reins, the pony didn't run off. Fearful I wouldn't, somehow I remounted and didn't know where the pony was heading. It was summer lightning all the way. We arrived home after 11 p.m.

1928-9

A new horseman was engaged, P., a youngish, strong, tall and active man coming from a horsy farm. He was to live in with us, the older horseman A. took on as cowman. The three young Shires were taking their place in the regular work. Three other horsemen, so-called, were tried. One I accidentally met a few years ago. "Here!" he said, "I know you. Your father had those three smart horses. I couldn't manage them." At least he was honest: the next one wasn't. After a short time he complained of a poisoned toe. An older man, he sat by our fire for a week. We asked to see his toe, but he refused, saying he was going to Plymouth to see his doctor the next day. He came back and sat by the fire again: he said he'd been told to rest it. Father became suspicious and asked the name of his doctor. In the end it came out that the rascal had no bad toe, he had just wrapped it up and had near a fortnight's holiday at our expense. Another pleasant enough young man, too easy going, came in a pair of light shoes, saying he had nothing else. Just think of trying, in shoes, to work those great shires on cobbled yards and ploughed fields. My father bought him a pair of hob-nailed boots, deducting a bit off his wages each week. He didn't stay long. P. stayed several years.

Those horses were so powerful and quick: turn their heads up any hill and they would run up to the top, if not held back, with whatever load behind. With all three in the reaper binder father had difficulty in holding them. The first round or two of a field they would run up the hill side of the field and not stop until their heads were over the top hedge. When there was more room, after a round or two, he would make me walk backwards in front of them, attempting to keep them back. I didn't like it for fear of being trampled. He knew on command they would stop dead.

These three were sufficient horses soon, as the corn price had dropped and there would be less arable. Father wisely seeded the old barley stubble gradually with a good permanent grasses and clover mixture. Nancy, Blossom and Punch were sold. Later, in turn, we heard Punch fell into the road from a high hedge, was injured and shot. Blossom was gored to death by a bull.

Chapter 8.
My Early Farming: From Winter to Summer.

By this stage I had watched and tried many jobs on the farm. Some were too intricate, some too heavy: simpler ones I could help with. Horses and waggons were in general use and a boy was always in demand to hold on to the horse or lead it along while the men loaded or unloaded the waggon.

Farming naturally is seasonal and sees a marked change from winter to summer. Briefly, winter is spent mostly looking after livestock. The horses cart hay, straw and roots constantly to need, and plough the fields, when weather suits, ready for Spring cultivation. Winter is time for repairing hedges, - much hand labour was spent necessarily on this laborious and profitless task on two counts: first, to secure your animals, and secondly by obligation to your tenancy agreement, as pre-war most farmers were tenants and fields smaller which increased hedge-length per farm. The standard method to repair a Devon hedge is to cut off all surplus growth except young saplings on top (if any) for relaying, using the wood for stakes or firewood. Then re-turfing the sides up to 5 ft. high before relaying saplings along the top for stock-proofing. Wet days or in freeze-ups there were numerous winter jobs in the barns.

The Spring brought the additional busy time of lambing and corn cultivation. The fields for corn were worked down from the ploughing until a suitable tilth was obtained. This meant walking on ploughing after your horses harrowing, rolling, ripping it up again, more harrowing and rolling, then sowing manure, and finally the seed. Day after day with continuous aching legs. I was glad to seek my feather bed at night in my young days.

All corn sowing was to be finished by May 1st or there would be loss of yield. May 1st is recognised as the dividing change to Summer, traditionally celebrated by national holiday and ancient customs like hobby horse days in North Devon and Cornwall. On the farm it signified the end of laborious winter feeding, when all stock can be turned out to grass, except in fields required to grow on to be cut for hay later.

Our village celebrated May 1st with our school dancing the maypole. We were invited to one big house or another to dance on the lawn. The girls, all dressed in white, my sisters included, had coloured ribbons drawn through their fronts, matching the coloured braids on the pole - a pretty scene. After, were tea and games.

Jobs in May.

But, back on the farm, like after the Lord Mayor's show comes the dung cart. For now with all the stock turned out to grass in May. any dung remaining piled up in yards and sheds was carted out to the fields. It was pitched by hand onto the carts, raked out into small heaps across the field, then spread evenly with hand forks, and finally ploughed in as fertiliser for the last of the arable crops in that spring. The soil was worked down to a fine 'tilth' for mangel, turnips and kale. May was not too late for planting potatoes, earlier was better. The corn crops were already up and growing, the right stage for rolling and a light harrowing to invigorate tillering (root growth). Lambing was finished except for a few 'cuckoo' lambs. Another dirty job was tail-docking sheep, that is clipping the dirty wool from round their backsides, preferably done in April before the flush spring grass opened their bowels to make them messier.

May too was gull nesting time, for me and other boys. Thousands nested on our cliffs among other birds. Despite warnings not to go climbing cliffs, I could not resist and spend many hours in that exciting environment. With other boys we collected gulls' eggs (legal then), lit a fire and boiled them in a tin. One Whitsun, on the highest point of our cliffs, four of us saw a couple bathing in a secluded cove below. Then, unaware of us, we watched how a couple in the nude can enjoy themselves. Stating it was a bit shameful, one boy in disgust threw an egg down, it hit a rock and splashed all over them. Immediately the rest of us followed, and emptied our basket in a continuous spray on the luckless couple. We were home across the fields before they could have recovered. I was nine to ten years old at the time.

Haymaking.

Hay was the first crop harvested, that is grass, when fully grown, cut and dried by sun and wind, then to be conserved in stacks for winter animal fodder - a very important crop. From Mid-summer through July the proverb "Make hay while the sun shines" became a reality. When the hay was raked, dried and in pooks the boys' job was to lead the horse from pook to pook while the men with pitch forks heaved it to the man making the load on the waggon. The full load was then taken to the stack and the hay pitched off on top to the stack builders.

Orders to the boy were: "Never move off without shouting 'Hold on,' or a sudden start may jerk the man off the waggon," and "Look out for your own toes." It only took once for a heavy Shire to plant his foot on yours to learn that was good advice.

In the late 1920s a new tool, the hay sweep, gathered the dried hay in the field, like a large kind of rake, pulled by a horse, and a considerable load could be dragged to the stack, thus saving hand-pitching to waggons. We became adept in its use. But there was still some hand pitching at the stack, and from ground level.

Horse-hoeing and Hand-hoeing of Root Crops.

Contemporary with haymaking was the hoeing of root crops. That is the weeding and singling plants to suitable spacings. Mangels, turnips, swedes and kales are the usual crops dealt with in this manner. A three-row horse-drill guided across a field will plant three rows of seed spaced about 22" - 24" apart. The rate of seed flow is adjustable. As soon as the seed has germinated and the rows can be seen plainly, with the weather dry, the crop is horse-hoed (scuffled). That is a tool with hoe blades set to follow the seed drill. It hoes the weeds BETWEEN the rows. Someone leads the horse and another person at the rear guides the hoe by two handles. The someone leading the horse between the rows is often a boy, who must try not to let the horse step on the plants.

The two jolly workers who singled (hoed)
4 acres of swedes in a day

Of all the persecuted there's none like a chastised scuffle boy. "Can't you see?" "Keep to the left." "You're going too fast." "His left hind foot is stepping on the plants." "Are you asleep? Can't you see that stinging bee is making him wobble. Stop and kill it with your hat." A thankless task - which was repeated about three times per field. Was I glad when promoted to the rear handles!

Hand hoeing was weeding and singling the plants IN the rows, that commenced at about the four leaf stage. At mid-summer crops grew quickly, often gangs of men hoed before the crop outgrew them. But woe betide the man if the boss found the smallest weed or double plants. Some men liked the job and became fast and skilful. I hated the job: my eyes watered with concentration, especially in the wind, and the plants became blurred. Our horseman and one of the Bevell family, when younger, took on contract hoeing by the acre. Starting at 4 a.m., they rested again at mid-day when their wives brought food, then worked again until 8 p.m. They slept in a tent. One day they singled (there was no weed) 4 acres of swedes. Years later in an adjoining field I achieved my best with three others, - four acres of swedes in two days, between milkings. My uncle G. hoed a 13-acre field of swedes in 14 days.

Through Hoeing to Kingsbridge Fair and the Corn Harvest.

All root hoeing was expected to be finished by Kingsbridge Annual Fair at the end of July, with the threat that you couldn't attend it otherwise. Another ruse to promote faster work. I never knew the threat carried out in my time. Everyone reckoned to spend some time enjoying the excitement of this yearly three-day event. On the Thursday was the big cattle and sheep market with brisk business for the farmers. At this fair always was heard from farmers, to suggest that they were 'early birds', mention that they had cut a field of oats at home. Boasting, unseemingly of course, just a casual mention, for it was extremely early to start harvest, but the hint got through. I've known a farmer cut into an unripe field for the sake of it. The pleasure fair continued until Saturday night.

Scything down the corn, and then tying the sheaves by hand stopped with the advent of horse reapers, and then the reaper binder which completed both operations. My father had helped scythe whole fields, but bought his first reaper binder about 1910.

In my time we only scythed around the edges of fields so the horses with the machine on the first round did not tread out the grain. Also we scythed steep areas where the machine couldn't get, or badly laid crops. Or we used scythes to control and tidy fields of bracken, thistles and weeds, annually. When hay grass was scythed as well it needed a continuously sharp tool, because grass grows thicker and is tougher than less thick corn.

Summer advanced into August, the month of ripening the golden corn. As a boy I helped prepare the reaper-binder, oiling, checking, changing the wheels for roads and back again to working position in the field. I fetched and carried to order, helped stook the cut corn, spread the sheaves to wind and sun, restooked as necessary until the sheaves were dry enough to be carted and ricked.

I watched and learned how to pitch sheaves the correct way to the waggon while leading the horse from stook to stook. On our steep fields when turning a waggon the order came: "Don't turn too sharply or the waggon will tip over." I wasn't strong enough to control Shires with minds of their own. Over the waggon would go, and there would be curses while the men reloaded. Sooner or later, when there was a man short, "You jump on the waggon and load, boy, I'll pitch up." And so I learned how to load a waggon. Later I got a reputation for building large loads.

F.W. Snowdon's reaper binder, c. 1912

Then one day the usual: "We're a man short, you will have to learn to 'turn sheaves'." That is, to stand on the rick, take every sheaf that is thrown up from the waggon and turn it stubble end forward to drop beside the rick-builder. This was for his convenience to quickly place the sheaves round the outside of the stack (rick) so that the grain in the ear end of the sheaves is kept dry towards the rick centre. Each outside round is then bound in place by an inner round halfway across the first, and another until the middle is full. He proceeds on the outside again until the stem of the rick is high enough. Then each row is brought in a bit to form the roof for thatching.

There are several waggon loads in a stack, thousands of sheaves. My arms were dropping off by nightfall. It was manly to stick it. After a few years of that repetition I learned how to control sheaves on a bouncy stack and eventually to be a master rick-builder.

The Wonder of the Harvest.

I knew that I would be dwelling to write about harvest time, that richest and most colourful scene in the year, and other than the practical, with my romanticism for the natural scene. As a toddler walking for the first time ever into a field of corn cutting, with a child's first impression of a new experience, I was awed in wonder. Mabel was leading me with one hand and carrying tea for the men in the other. The beauty of that dimensional and colourful picture before me registered for ever.

Since, to walk along a high-hedged Devon lane, hanging with August greenery and flowers, then to turn into a field of golden corn just being cut never failed to excite me. Rows of neatly tied sheaves led to the wall of uncut corn, and the horses in the reaping machine passed by on another round silhouetted against a clear blue sky.

I longed for it each year, and as a small boy helped to get the reaper-binder started off. I watched as the three dark bay horses set off, contrasted against the yellow corn. The machine clacked along, kicking out sheaves regularly in lines, and disappeared over the hill. Left alone in silence I sat on a sheaf, but nature was not still. By our disturbance butterflies, bees, insects, and beetles filled the ambience, in the air, on the foliage, finding a new place to settle. On the wall of corn, which looked like a layer cake of yellows and tans, hung a large green grasshopper, slowly adjusting its hold. A harvest mouse, scared out of its ball of straw nest, clung trembling to the corn straws by toes and curled tail. A hen pheasant stalked out and guided her young brood to the safety of the hedge. A rabbit hopped out and back again. Among the corn blazed a scarlet poppy and rich blue cornflowers. Near ground level in the stubble chinked the little yellow and purple wild pansy. The pleasant smell of crushed wild mint invaded the air.

The clacking binder returned in its urgency and broke the spell of my reverie. "Fetch me another ball of twine by next round!" The struggle of all for survival.

To all grain farmers the corn harvest was the crowning glory of the year, a culmination of the year's planning and endeavour. Now was the big sweat against the weather to save as much grain as possible in as good condition as possible. For tenant farmers the result could decide whether they remained in the farm. Harvest was easier in

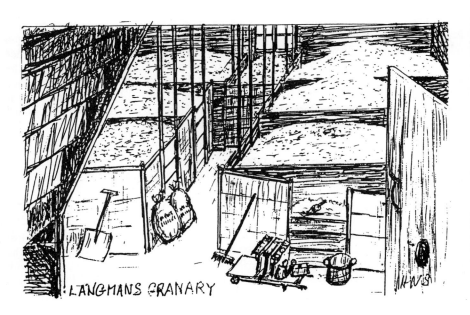

LANGMANS GRANARY

a fine spell of weather, but there could be no let up in our unpredictable climate. Having several attempts to dry it in catchy weather is also tiring, and it is depressing to watch the grain deteriorating. We toiled on to the finish. It was a great challenge to keep fit, on top, and secure a good harvest. I loved it, not having the personal worry, and in our long summer school holidays too.

As I grew older and did more there was more tiredness, evenings, but a good supper of ham, fat pork, fried potatoes, pickled onions, apple pie and cream put us to right. Father liked to finish harvest before school started again.

Autumn

Corn harvest usually ran into Autumn before the fields were clear allowing the stubbles to be ripped up and burned clearing weeds and disease (not straw burning, a bad practice). A very familiar autumn scene was little smoking fields everywhere, like garden bonfires. But there were still crops to be harvested. First, potatoes matured in banked rows in the fields were dug out by hand with a 2 or 3 toed digger. October was the ideal time. Usually taking 3 rows at a time potatoes were selected by hand as dug and thrown into baskets one for wore (good) and one, scruff (small and damaged). Also a third basket of seed (good egg sized) was saved. Baskets were emptied into sacks for storage in cellars, or for sale, or clamped in the field, that is tipped into a heap, then covered with straw for insulation and also six inches of soil on top to keep out light and frost.

Secondly November, ideal for harvesting mangels, a large beet full of sugar. They were pulled by hand, shook off the leaves and into rows wide enough for horse and cart to drive between. Then thrown into the carts by hand and drawn off to a sheltered position where they, susceptible to frost, were clamped in a large heap, to be covered with straw and hedge parings a foot thick. From Christmas until May they were fed to stock. They are now considered a hard labour crop and little grown.

This leaves the apple crop harvested October - November. Those required for hoarding for eating and cooking, are carefully picked off the trees from ladders avoiding bruising from which they rot. For cider that doesn't matter, and fallen ones are picked from the ground and bagged to go to the press. Late apples are knocked from the trees with poles.

Pig Killing.

The local pig-killer came to farms to kill pigs in numbers for marketing, or singly for home consumption. The pig was stuck in the throat with a sharp knife to kill and bleed it. (Later by law it was to be stunned first with a humane killer).

Before deep freezers it was seasonal (like oysters). Kill only with an 'R' in the month, the colder ones, because that was safer with the cures available. Usually the house pig was killed in November, before Christmas and another one in April.

After the pig was killed boiling water was poured over the carcass to sterilize it which also allowed the hair to be scraped off with a thin layer of outer skin. Then it was hung up, the belly was cut out and made into luxury hogs pudding later and there would be fresh liver for supper.

Next day the meat, cut up, was immersed in cold 'brine' that is salt boiled in water then cooled, which stored and preserved it. A little salt-petre was first rubbed into the

PIG KILLING
H.N.S.

lean meat, otherwise it hardened. Before cooking the salt was soaked out in cold water, but the lean retained much salt. That is why fat pork was preferred, delectable when roast, boiled, or fried, a staple farm diet, much despised today. And why pigs were fattened up with as much as 4 inches of back fat, which was cut off the lean and cooked separately.

Chapter 9.
Kingsbridge Grammar School.

I was to start at Kingsbridge Grammar School aged 11 years on September 20th, 1929. I was to cycle the five miles, but I had no cycle, nor had I ever ridden one. I was worried. Father had walked the four miles from Clanacombe to school daily. I always suspected that he toyed with the idea that I should walk. I acquainted him with my predicament. Meanwhile, our butcher's son, one year older than me, whom I played with often, had an old bike rusting and without tyres in their orchard. With his consent, I tried to ride it. My father came across me riding it. "Looks like you're managing very well," he said. Two days before school he took me to Plymouth by bus and bought a Hercules cycle for me at £3.19.6d. A carrier van delivered it to Churchstow and we walked it 2½ miles home.

Next day I practised on it, let it fall over and bent the crank. P., our new horseman, a cyclist himself, noticed. "You've let that new bike fall over and bent the crank!" Next day I rode it to school and coming home tried to ride it up a steep hill, like the other boys, and, falling off, was nearly run over by a chauffeur-driven car. I became adept and cycled everywhere, often to escape the farm work when I could. I won races at sports - I was specially good in the slow bicycle races, a popular event.

Thoughts before entering Kingsbridge Grammar School.

My young years had passed through innocence, play, make belief, selfishness, and was changing more to awareness and reality: that one could not always have one's way, one had to think, share and help more. I learned growing up to become a man that could stick work, that even muscles and bones ached. I was eleven years old, becoming more involved with the farm, willingly or on command.

I loved our valley, knowing every inch of it from Clanacombe to the sea. When the farm men were away in the fields I grasped all the time to range it. The stream in the bottom ran both sides of a hedge to water properties either side. The hedge was well wooded, and, in summer, semi-tropically overgrown in verdure. There was abundant bird, animal and plant life. I loved to stalk that hedge through gardens, orchards and meadows without being seen. I could roam the fields on the hills, explore woods, cliffs and the

Hubert Snowdon aged 11 years ready to set out for KGS

beach. Seldom challenged as a trespasser, accepted as a villager. West Buckland valley, a beautiful rural haven, described by a Salcombe author as "the place God made next to Heaven." Completely happy in that lone side of my life I never wanted to leave.

As the day for Kingsbridge Grammar School (KGS) approached mixed feelings grew in intensity. Fears for the new disciplines: to face them or opt out? The latter was predominant, wishing I was old enough to leave school to work on the farm. The alternative was to cycle to Kingsbridge Modern Secondary School. To go there would be loss of pride after winning a Grammar School place.

As I saw Kingsbridge Grammar School, for my supposed betterment, the wholesome village life that I enjoyed was to be pricked by pale-faced townee academics, by book learning, abhorred by country folk who left school with little but the three R's, some before their teens, and who became the successful backbone of farms and village, going along with nature and the good earth sufficiently for life. I wished to emulate these giants. Other than the obvious there were disciplines: - cycling 5 miles every morning, wearing clean clothes, new etiquette, answering the "poshly" spoken, being lured to soft indoor life from our fresher outdoors. Fear of these panged my stomach. So I numbed myself and drifted towards the inevitable.

Thoughts on entering Kingsbridge Grammar School.

A grammar school education was believed the best available. I entered Kingsbridge Grammar School (founded 1672) on 29th September 1929, and could not have described my feelings adequately. Now that past education and 67 years more of life will have influence, but I attempt to remember it. From my rural home I had never travelled farther than to Dartmoor and Plymouth on a Sunday school treat.

Quoting the adage "A little knowledge is dangerous," I doubted and feared where this upper education would lead me in the wide world. I felt that I was entering a club of learning established so long ago, so old, seeming without change, that it could not be challenged. Older than its panelled halls, like our drab and depressing example, with traditions stretching back to the founders, ancient Greeks, and its cupboards gathering fustiness over centuries that dared not be opened to question.

I found our masters, achievers in the club via university, wore seriously that funny black hat and flowing dress-like cloak as a symbol of academic success. I soon learned that Plato, Archimedes, Pythagoras and co.'s philosophies initiated the system. I learned that cricket played in white clothes, with two batsmen at the same time at two wickets, queerly moulded boys to believe in fair play; that the three R's were subdivided into arithmetic, algebra, geometry, trigonometry; English into composition, literature and poetry, plus Latin, Greek and French; science into physics, chemistry and heat; that there was a place called infinity where a circle becomes a straight line; that in decimals one hundred divided by three has no answer except at infinity; that also, not surprisingly perhaps, there is a strong belief in Greek mythology.

Good stories, but who will they feed? Older boys than me from our village going through KGS came away with somewhat superior attitudes. Never did I see one in the field helping to save the harvest, like many of our willing villagers. That concerned me. Could I honour the Grammar School? Everybody must eat, farming is a necessity to life. What changed those lads? These are some of my thoughts remembered, more later. Finally, another adage: "Don't despise the hand that feeds you!"

I settled in with what I couldn't avoid, partially resentful, first, at having to take home 1½ hours prep., later 2 hours. Several raven frocked teachers with varying dispositions controlled us. Some ruled by cane - the fear of it was always there. In monthly tests I usually finished in the bottom half of the class. We country boys clanned up against the town boys and showed our frustrations when let out by rustic behaviour, nearly as bad as at Thurlestone school.

At home, after a while, I was routed out of bed and told to be in the cowshed when the men started at 7 a.m., to milk two cows by hand, then feed some pigs, fill up some milk bottles, have my breakfast, and with my bicycle push the bottles of milk up steep Clanacombe hill to deliver at a guest house - as much as twenty pints in summer. Then I had to ride the rest of the five mile at school by 9 a.m. Sundays and holidays, except for going on to school, I did the same.

After cycling home by 4.30 p.m. I was expected to milk again, and help finish the yard work by the usual 6 p.m. tea. After this I did my homework. I dodged that milking as often as I dared, with the excuse that I had to play football or other games. Actually, it was voluntary after school.

My first caning came wrongfully. Myself and another boy next to me both had the same answer, and wrong. I was not the copier, and was upset. Two strokes across the backside each. No Solomon's judgment here, without a baby, to prevail.

HWS

Later Visitors.

At home by 1930, my first long summer holiday from K.G.S., the visitor business had increased, especially in summer as more people afforded holidays and farther afield. As well as transport by G.W.R. to its advertised "Holiday Haunts" they came increasingly by motor car to where ever they chose, in Fords, Austins, Bull-nosed Morris, M.G.s, even Trojans and Baby Austins. Usually they were from London and southern areas, seldom

Site of secret Z under felled poplar tree

was a north country accent heard. They arrived exhausted, dusty, with radiators boiling, and luggage, even passengers, outside in the 'dickie' seat. The journey was quite an ordeal in 1930.

At the farm visiting children soon paired up with us in respective ages. The greatest attraction always was Bantham beach, with the farm a close second. They alternated between the two. We joined them when allowed freedom from our chores. At times they helped us. In August whole families came for a fortnight, some for the whole month. They loved the ponies, and next the ripening apples in the orchards. They brought portable gramophones to our delight, with all the 1920's tunes. We played it in the summer house, where also they taught us a game, "Priest of the Parish." We played it at every chance, adults and all.

Invited to go fishing, I had to ask permission from my father. Yes, as long as you are back by mid-day to go harvesting." He had a very shrill whistle with his fingers between his teeth, and the whole village knew that meant I had to run home from wherever.

My third sister and her mate devised a secret, named it Z, and for three years or more kept it despite our enquiring. It was discovered by accident. Men cutting out a mass of brambles grown over a fallen poplar tree against a dry hedge found a rustic hut completed with a galvanised roof. At first it was thought the lair of a tramp, but childish feminine contents gave away the game. The poplar tree was one of many cut down by Hutchings and Cave in the 1920's.

Jealous, in opposition, I made my own secret. Unknowingly my site was under a branch of that same huge poplar tree over a hedge ten yards away. I buried a large cloam pipe in which I hid forbidden treasures, penknives, catapults, arrows and spears. It may be there still.

A Room with a View.

A place especially enjoyed and remembered by visitors and family alike was the window seat in the large bedroom over the kitchen. The room, itself light and airy, had pale primrose oil canvas spattered with green horse-shoe wreaths and red flowers on the floor. The walls were warmer, nearer to beige, and all reflected sunshine. There were three beds and usual furnishing, with a few rush mats spread here and there.

There was more than the pleasant view across the valley described earlier. One could sit there alone with a sense of security, yet not alone, because underneath were family sounds of a busy kitchen, and one was aptly situated for hearing and seeing outside approachers to front and back door. Those to the front scrunched gravel, those to the back were announced by the loud click of the yard door, and a cautious glance revealed who came and went. Some conversations could not be helped being overheard.

Inside the house the room could be again approached by front or back stairs, allowing a quick exit by either door if required. But we were a happy family in those early days and willing to share.

The feeling engendered by the chance situation of that room is difficult to describe. Imagine viewing from the open window in spring and summer as one above, not of power, but of family watchfulness, part guardian of home, and with one's own reveries.

New School, 1931.

I was taught in three Kingsbridge Grammar schools. The original buildings of 1640, now a museum, at 20 Fore Street, previously a nunnery, and the new school built at Westville in 1931, now Comprehensive. We were to walk there in single file. Like now, with a national depression, a lorry could not be afforded to transport our books. The head asked for suggestions. "Carry them ourselves, Sir," I piped up. "What! Books and papers littered along the streets?" "No, Sir, in a sack, Sir." "There! Of course," cried the Head "is the answer." And he flew off to a sack merchant. I was in his good books for common sense evermore. "Why didn't I think of it?" he asked as we marched off.

At the new school our fourth form was temporarily housed next to the Headmaster's study, because our room was not finished. Then it was right down the other end of the corridor, past the art room stairs, behind the boiler room, isolated. Shut away there for our second year in the fourth form, which meant repetition mostly copied from last years' books, we became known as the worst form ever, and lived up to it! Unruly, still opposing discipline, by which, as so often happens in life, we contributed to our own problems. My problems piled up, deserved or not. More sensitive underneath than my outwards burliness, unaware, I pressed on doggedly into trouble just like children do.

At a critical age, 13-14 years, and growing fast, I was expected to work hard at home and at school. Continually, for bad work I was given detentions, half an hour of work after school. Arriving late for school a second time the head prefect gave me a week. A master I feared also gave me a week, and masters rarely doling out detentions dolloped them on me in twos and threes. I amassed 20 detentions in one day, surely a record. Notified, the Head gave me two strokes to wipe out the prefect's week. Saturday afternoon I sat in his dining room 3 hours and worked off six. More at home on Sunday. The rest, as I could, let off none.

The prep one evening was to learn a Shakespeare sonnet, just fourteen lines. I could not manage, even with my sister's help. By the morning I could only repeat four lines. My concentration was little, my brain closing down for a rest. I became melancholic.

The master I feared was nicknamed Joey, and we had him for two periods following history and algebra on Tuesday mornings. I dreaded going to school that day, and would have liked to have played hookey, but Snowdons weren't quitters. I never lost a day in five years except for illness and our annual Sunday School outing. Joey received his nickname supposedly because he bore a hooked nose resembling a parrot. He was hard on boys our age. To see him walk into the classroom, always in his black gown, jaw dropped, cane in one hand and a pile of prep. books under the other arm, our hearts sank. Who was for it? He had blue-pencilled my prep all over, obviously in temper. He gave me and other boys four strokes each - the most I ever had. I did not attract the cane but a few times at school.

Three weeks later, when bathing with some boys at Bantham beach, when wiping down, one boy exclaimed "Oh! Look at those marks on your back side. You've had the cane at school." Blue marks were still showing after three weeks.

Whatever a boy deserved, I don't think beating will make him want to learn. That want will come when he is ready.

My underlying unhappiness came to be noticed. One day the Head happened to meet me in the corridor. "Snowdon," he said, "You look ill! Go home!" My parents didn't understand, nor did I quite. They took me to the doctor, who couldn't find anything wrong. "His nerves are a bit jumpy, let him skip school for a bit." I was annoyed. I would miss the school sports at which last year I won our house cup with the most points, at a young age. I stayed at home six weeks and ran wild. Then I returned to school to pick up the threads, and, as usual after a holiday, my backside itched for three or four days sitting on wooden forms all day.

Recently, at a KGS annual re-union dinner which I have not attended for more than 30 years - and I am one of the oldest old boys now - Joey was praised to the highest. He should have been headmaster" was voiced. "The cane didn't hurt us, the discipline of the school had fitted us for posts all over the world." It did. Later in the higher forms Joey was very interesting, especially in history. I maintain he wasn't fit to teach younger boys. Too hard, I shall never forgive him.

The English master one day said "Snowdon, it's time you started shaving." My father always shaved with a cut-throat razor and persuaded me to try it, but it didn't suit. I was given a new safety razor for my thirteenth birthday, and soon was shaving daily.

Incidentally, that same cut-throat razor we used to castrate young pigs on the farm. About 12 years of age I was made to hold the piglets and watch how their testicles were cut out. The first time I felt a little queer, but I came to do it myself later. For colts, calves and lambs we engaged a vet, who cauterised the wounds with a hot iron. Later advanced methods meant we could perform this ourselves.

Veterinary practice advanced in technique more than any other branch of agriculture, especially eased by hypodermic needle and anaesthetic. Before, the vet on arrival would ask "How many men have you got handy?" If necessary, with large animals, men roped and held down the poor 'critter' until the vet in cold blood finished.

The 'Z' girls with Jessie

Chapter 10.
Grandfather Snowdon.

Grandfather Snowdon was a sturdy thick-set man, feared God and very little else. He spoke little, but much to the point when needed. Through my childhood he helped on the farm at busy times, like the threshing. In 1919 when helping to thresh barley for the outgoing tenant at Buckland Farm, and 55 years of age, he pitched every sheaf from the rick up to the threshing machine that day. Twenty tons of barley grain were threshed and with the weight of straw added he must have pitched near double that weight. He told me later that by that evening it was the first time he felt done in by a day's work.

Another contemporary of his, a Moore, somewhere relative to my mother, also a wonderful craftsman who had taught my father much, told me himself that he was 53 years of age before he ever felt tired. It says something for going to bed at 8 p.m. and rising at 4 a.m. with plenty of fresh air and fresh food I suspect.

Grandfather always wore a bowler hat, and one day walking under the thresher driving belt it was knocked off and his badly cut head had to be stitched. He liked ferreting for rabbits and taught me. Taking a rabbit from a net one day he broke its neck, he thought, as usual, and threw it to the ground. Seconds later the rabbit got up and head one-sided ran up the field. Thwarted, Grandfather shouting ran, but losing out threw his bowler at it, all to no avail. He didn't like to lose a rabbit.

He grew our vegetables in the garden, and taught me. He was swinging an axe with the men in his seventies "keeping them at it," cutting off the orchard hedge. I was on one end of the cross-cut saw when cutting up the big wood. How my arms ached! With age, he became a little crafty. He and I, age 12-13 years, were to take a cow to the bull, up to the farm through Thurlestone village by the church. He helped me through the first crossroads, then said, "There you are, boy, get on with it." He turned tail and went home. I had to run about on my own. The bull was running with cows over several fields and kept himself between me and our cow, serving her as often as he could. I could not part them, and with no-one in sight I did not relish having to come between a bull and his wives. I stuck to it, chasing them miles and eventually got away. I never told anyone.

After Grandmother Snowdon died, on 12th March 1932 at 74 years, he came to live with us at Langmans, but did not get on well with my mother. He blamed her for bringing his son down by having six children.

One Saturday at mid-day dinner of roast beef, when he noticed how much I ate he remarked "The butcher will need to kill a bullock a week to keep you."

He was having words with mother one morn, and when he went out I asked her what that was about. She, a cat lover, replied "He doesn't like the way the cats are scratching the legs of his table." As I was unaware it was his table, she told me there was a story attached. Catching him at a quiet moment, I asked. It happened to be the solid working table in the centre of our kitchen, about 5' 6" x 3' top, with two drawers. "Well," he said,

"I found a plank of pine washed up on Lea's Foot beach, and there wasn't a knot in it. I carried it upon my back up to my brother Harry's workshop." That was at least a quarter of a mile up hill, where Harry Snowdon had a workshop and sawpit opposite the Old Rectory gate. "He made me that table out of half the plank and was to make me a wardrobe out of the other, but I never got that one." I asked, "Well, water sodden, how heavy was that plank?" "About four hundredweight!" he replied. Possibly exaggerated a little, but these were phenomenal feats. A man for a bet on Kingsbridge quay was reputed to have carried half a ton across the gang plank onto the packet boat. Another attempted to carry a two-hundredweight sack from Widecombe to Postbridge on Dartmoor, but failed on an upward slope. How much did the silent Snowdons hide? When asked, often the answer was "You know nothing about it, boy."

Occasionally Grandfather liked to wander off. When it took his fancy he would set off on foot as the crow flies across fields, the shortest route, to meet old friends or to some event, whether it was two miles or ten. He took a lift with a carrier or whoever if it suited. This he had done all his life, I learned.

Our marvellous blacksmith, Ingram, in W. Buckland, shoed our horses and mended our tools. If a man carried a broken tool to him going home in the evening, Ingram would start his forge at 4 a.m. and mend the tool for the man to take to work in the morn. He had a son retired from Navy who became our cobbler. When too old he retired to London with, in turn, his son of the Metropolitan Police, the KGS boy who spoke with my eldest sister. The cobbler wrote back to W. Buckland some of his memories, including the following: Because his blacksmith father put up the price of shoeing by a halfpenny a shoe, old Bill Snowdon (my grandfather) complained and took his horses to South Milton, a mile or two farther away.

In 1933 grandfather, with us at Langmans, rose a bit earlier than usual, scrubbed his bearded face round at the kitchen sink, snatched a quick breakfast and disappeared. He came back later grinning and told us he had been up in an aeroplane. It happened Sir Allen Cobham had brought his "Flying Circus" to a field behind our church. Grandfather and another old villager, Jack Ellis, were the first two up. One of my twin sisters won a free flight. I personally hated the noise and wouldn't go near. In fact in the evening I went to Bantham Undercliff for a swim, where the high cliffs drowned out the noise.

Aging beyond work, grandfather liked to walk to Bantham and with other old cronies sit on the seat by the beach gate overlooking the river. They eyed and criticised the visitors in their scanty beach wear, otherwise aggravated one another. "Why do you always tell them it's going to be fine, when you know to-day it will rain?" "They don't want to know that, do they."

On 26th October 1933, aged 78, he gave up completely, went to bed for a fortnight, thanked his son Frank, my father, and died fearing to meet his God.

Chapter 11.
Farm and School, 13-16 years.

At Easter and Christmas school holidays, age 13-15 years, my job after milking, milk round and chores, was to take horse and cart out to the turnip fields or the mangold clamp and load up to draw the roots out for the sheep and outlying cattle. Once in their field the horse was let wander across the field, while I flung the roots off the cart by hand. By this time I was using Prince, the youngest Shire, the maddest goer of the lot, but obedient to the word, and on the word "go" he'd rush off like a train. In fact I dragged the wheel with a chain and left it on, uphill or down, in attempt to slow him. He had to be watched all the time in case he charged straight through a gap in a hedge or gateway.

This occupied me several days a week, two or three loads out to the fields and a load home for cattle and horses at the farm. Often we had a double dose on Saturdays because we didn't work the horses on Sunday.

On the other days I was taking the second waggon after the horseman out to the ricks for hay and straw to bring it into the barns for cattle and horses. He would cut out the hay with the big knife and pitch it onto the waggons for me to make the loads. Soon he complained at having to cut and pitch both loads to a big boy like me. So I had to cut and pitch one load to him - much harder. Then he was bored and anxious at the time taken because I was slow.

Sometimes village boys interested in farm life helped me. But I learned the truth of "two boys are half a boy" when we arrived home late after fooling around. I found father waiting for the next job, and he boxed my ears. There were other seasonal jobs we helped with when, as fitting, the other men would draw the roots such as at Easter potato planting, or at Christmas poultry plucking, or grinding corn in the barn on wet days, or evenings, for the incessant demands of cows and horses.

On Sundays we were expected to attend Sunday school or the chapel service at least once for the day.

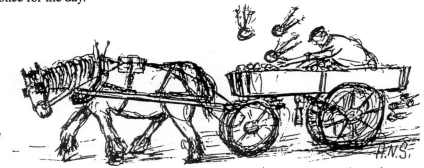

PRINCE PULLING WAGGON WITH CHAINED WHEEL

CUTTING HAY FROM RICK TO LOAD ON WAGGON

Hay Knife Tragedy.

Incidentally, having mentioned hay knives, a school pal of mine just left school at 15 years old, the same age as me, cut himself accidentally on the leg with one. Tragically he died of blood poisoning. We had cycled to school together, were in the same form, had worked and played together, and visited each other's farms, rabbiting or whatever. The whole school marched to his funeral and lined the church paths. I was asked to be a bearer, - it would be understood if I refused. I accepted, feeling very reluctant, yet dutifully obliged as his family, (with five girls and he the only boy, the same as mine) had asked for it. It was the least I must do. Stunned, the reality was a young human death. My active pal would be in a coffin next to me, ever stilled. I had to be a man and felt a very small boy. It was not death I feared. On the farms we were used to animal deaths, - he and I had caused some. I feared that, at my first unrehearsed act as bearer, of upsetting the reverence and dignity required of the occasion by making mistakes or a fool of myself. It was managed, but a sad, sad occasion.

Never more than once at school was I asked what I thought of doing on leaving. Caught on the hop put me thinking quickly and seriously. If I had said 'farming' they would have tried to deter me from it, or, their interest in me would have finished. Thinking academically, with art as my best subject, I replied 'architecture' or 'the Metropolitan Police.' The latter was because a former KGS boy from our village had joined it, and when home was paying attention to my oldest sister. I thought he looked very smart.

Many years later, after my father's death, an aunt told me that he was horrified at the thought of losing my labour. He never said so to me. He apparently gained the

49

information through a letter from the school discussing my future. I know that after I left school he received a letter asking me back.

School Reports.

There was always guilt taking home school reports, but re-reading them now they aren't so bad. I don't recall much said about them at home. There were the usual masters' comments: "Could do better." "Doesn't try hard enough." and "Satisfactory."

I was only ever top of the class for Art, and took home several form prizes. I was a slow learner, but something stuck. Once I gained 91 marks out of 100 for the Geometry end of term exam. Noses were turned up, suggesting that I must have cheated. My nose was exceedingly put out. It was the easiest exam that I could have set myself. Another boy was top and praised for getting 99½% (marks.)

Never once in my five years at KGS did my father attend any school function or appear to have interest in any work I did there, or for prep. at home. I feel that he believed he could teach me most that was needed for farming. I admit that our evolved system was near perfected and sustainable, in balance with nature.

One Wednesday afternoon returning from market, he passed our sports field where we were running a half mile race. Opportunely, he watched through the hedge. After tea at home he told me, declaring that he thought me a very strong runner. Remembering the race, I know that I was 50 yards ahead of the field.

For religious instruction at school we were dividing the bible as literature into different sections, - history, stories, poetry etc. For prep. we had to make it up in rectangular grid form. I made mine up artistically, and in black and red, but a bit cramped. I still have it, intending to enlarge it. Discussing this with a sister, he overheard and took a look. "Oh! I didn't know they did anything like that at KGS," he said, surprised.

He himself preached on the Wesleyan local circuit earlier, but gave it up, I know, with great doubts on religious dogma, and out of his depth with thoughts on the subject. Our headmaster, also a great church man, showed doubt at times when taking us for religious instruction. Who doesn't have doubts?

School, 15-16 years.

There is no doubt that visitor children from different walks of life broadened our ex-school education, especially socially. We shocked one another at times in disbelief at the others' family protocol, taboos and expectancy for their children. However, those seemingly long halcyon summer days on the farm at harvest time, or on Bantham beach, came to an end in our mid-teens when they, our visitor pals, entered colleges and universities, with loftier ideas. But they never forgot. They revisited as adults to remember, some with their own children.

Meanwhile at school I left the wicked fourth form, raised to the lower and upper fifth forms, a change for the better. One lunch time I asked a farming friend to join us playing football. Reading a book, he refused. "No, I want to study." And that's how it became - we wanted to learn. No more caning - even Joey became interesting. Seriously working towards the Oxford School Certificate Examination, our brains were maturing towards full potential. We were happier and alert. We practised continually on old Certificate papers until the day came when the actual exam, for me, was just sitting another paper, with not too many butterflies in the tummy.

At sport I achieved well enough playing for the school 1st eleven in soccer and cricket, not regularly, a twelfth man for either. My prowess was long distance running. I won the coveted cross-country run in my last year, and was second in the previous year. In summer, somewhat guiltily, I succumbed to the Englishness of lazing on the boundary watching a school cricket match. We listened to other boys' poems, and discussed whether certain Twyford school girls had sex appeal. Those girls used our tennis courts in our playing field. Some did look pretty comely in their blue summer dresses. All strictly conventional by school rules. But boys did meet the girls after 4 p.m. in the local woods. The Headmaster found a love note written to a girl. He ordered the whole school to attend in the main hall at 4 p.m. one day. He read us a very, very conventional love story about a Miss Shepherd, who had lost her man. To what point I never knew. We still meet to-day survivors of those girls through the old pupils society, because the schools amalgamated to become Comprehensive and mixed.

Devon County Council Agricultural Classes.

While I was still at school Devon County Council (DCC) ran a three-year winter course on agriculture in the evenings weekly at KGS, for farmers and those interested. The tutor was Agricultural Advisor to DCC, a hard dour Scotsman. A Thurlestone farmer, who was at Langmans before us, offered to take father along. We had no car then. It turned out to be exceedingly interesting and informative, a comprehensive covering of the latest scientific finding in animal and crop husbandry. It resulted in father volunteering to grow trial plots of wheat, barley and mangolds for DCC, which decided for which varieties to grow of each. He was previously growing heavy crops. I remember seeing three mangolds, the largest ever, piled on our sack scales. I forget their weight, but the largest was as big as a bushel basket. People came from far around to see them.

There was a sneering at interfering CCs by tenant farmers who wished to be left alone. But neighbours soon asked "What manuring does DCC recommend?" They weren't told. There was justification for the antipathy of tenant farmers because CCs and Agricultural colleges seemed over-funded by government. Or whatever was recommended needed capital outlay which Devon tenant farmers had not. There was a saying: "If you want to ruin your son, send him to Agricultural College." Because he would come home with high-faluting ideas that couldn't be afforded, or would take an easier fixed-hours job, lost to that farm. There is a saying: "Farming with money comfortably is the way to lose it." The origin and whole basis of our farming was how to live off the land, regardless of the value of money. Now since the last war, rampant inflation with love of money the god, our traditional Devon sub-culture is dead. I dare mention the Lottery.

Hence father's fear of losing us by outside influence, not opposition to appropriate education.

The End of School.

Finally at school I sat the Oxford School Certificate Examination, finishing with painting on Saturday, midday, the 28th July 1934, my last day at school, and with another boy we celebrated at Kingsbridge Fun Fair that afternoon. The ancient annual cattle, horse and sheep fair, chartered centuries ago, was always the first Thursday after July 20th, and with all the traditional stalls, cheap-jacks selling every kind of paraphernalia, especially in season cherries and fairings (sugared almonds.)

In early times it was held in Fore Street and like a Bank Holiday everybody visited to enjoy it to the full. Farmers and workers with a very early start walked their animals to the sale before joining the revelry. In 1922 a new market was built and the animal Fair shifted there, extra to the weekly market. The sales increased, so that sheep and cattle were separated to two days and the fun fair carried on for three days to Saturday evening. Now the street fair has become a week of carnival attracting tourists.

For me it was home to work on the farm with my father as master and dominant figure, where his command and wishes were seldom opposed. I would like to have emulated him. He was an only son, not used to family competition, yet wished he had siblings and tried to be fairminded. A Victorian upbringing found him a silent and severe man, with the platitudes of his age, "Children should be seen and not heard." "Be a little man and stick it." and "You have to be cruel to be kind sometimes." When he approached, we watched his face to see how severe it was. He seldom praised, just said nothing; more likely criticised - "You know better than that." He expected more of us than we knew. He gave me, and others, an awful sense of guilt.

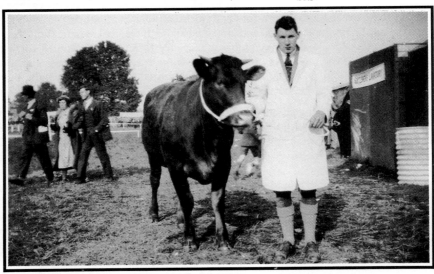

Hubert Snowdon with first prize South Devon heifer as member of
Kingsbridge YFC, shown at Devon County Show 1935-6

52

Yet he smiled at times, even joined in our fun. He liked to watch a bit of sport. Occasionally he would take a villager and myself in the pony trap on a Bank Holiday to a local football cup final. But mostly he worked very hard, was considered a good boss, and all who worked for him knew they would earn their money. He would not stand idlers.

I left school because I felt a man and ashamed to be there going on for 17 years of age and not earning my living. There was a career at home, a place I loved, and the work mostly learned without further ado.

Mother came to me one morning saying "They want you to go back to school." I replied "I'm not going." Father had received a letter with the request. He never mentioned it, but, 'like a man' that he was he had previously offered me the choice, to stay at home or go off, with the proviso "There is no more money to spend on you." And probably there wasn't. I felt peeved because I won the scholarship for a free Grammar School education. Otherwise it would have cost him full fees for two years at least, which was normal for farmers' sons, just so that they could state their sons had a Grammar School education. I cost him little, tenpence a day for wholesome cooked school dinners. For returning for a fifth helping once I was sent to the Head. He looked: "Never mind, you're a growing boy."

My dinners were offset by a bus allowance, but there never was a regular bus. There was some cost of sports gear, evening lectures, decent clothes, and a few extras not amounting to a lot.

He had to buy me another bicycle after I crashed one. He was not pleased. In his letter from the school there must have been reference to the Metropolitan Police. I don't know how else he could have known. For years after his death, discussing with an old aunt, she told me that he was horrified in case I left the farm, and he lost my labour.

My mother and aunts next door were wiser than my father in some things. They believed there was a better future me with my artistic talent and sensitive nature. They saw the hard work for little money that we imposed on ourselves. My mother hinted on my behalf at times, knowing of their own struggle, and what I was letting myself in for. But, always loyal to her gritty husband, she knew that at home I would ease his burden. She was often torn between decisions of her two men. My satisfaction was, and still is, in our fitness to produce necessary food, food for our nation. Money has little to do with it.

July 1934

My first job after school I remember was to help replace a post and wire fence. First we cut down some straight oak from our wood with cross-cut saw and axe then hauled it to our threshing barn with horses where a circular saw cut it to suitable sizes. The saw was driven by a 6½ horse-power Ruston Hornsby stationary engine bought in 1928 and the only mechanical device on the farm. It also drove an Albion grinding and rolling mill, and a barn thatching reed comber. I was used to working these machines before leaving school.

Simpler tools that we used to put the posts in were a Devon shovel, a very versatile tool, and a heavy hurdle iron bar. The bar was made by an Aveton Gifford blacksmith in 1908 for my father when he started farming at Pond Farm. "There you are my boy", said the blacksmith, "that one will last you a lifetime". It did. Two years after my father died in 1953 it broke in half with metal fatigue having banged down to many hurdles and fencing posts. I had it joined again for the old man's sake and I still have it. When small and with my father fencing sheep in turnips using hurdles, he would carry hurdles up the field and urge me to hurry after him with the bar-iron. I could hardly lift it so dragged it. On frosty mornings it stuck to my fingers. It was a 'man's' tool.

In some years there was a lull in July between hay and corn harvests, a good time for odd jobs like mending fences and gates. It was good practice to pare round corn field hedges, by hand, which allowed a clean start to corn-cutting when ripe. Otherwise the annual growth from the hedges tangled into the corn. The hedge parings would dry out a little and be used for rick bedding by the time the corn was harvested in August.

1934 was the height of the agricultural depression when like the present time, it was difficult to know where to turn some money. We were down to just four fields of corn, imported grain was very cheap. Thankfully our increasing milk round and summer visitors probably kept us going when some farms were going derelict.

With my oldest sister and self at home we were able to rear many more calves and increase our stock. The second sister went to Plymouth as governess to a doctor's children. The third sister was home for a time then was engaged as manageress of the dairy department for Buckfastleigh Co-op. The twins were still at school, now bussed daily to Kingsbridge Modern Secondary School.

With the girls doing the milk round I had time to dig our large walled garden by hand from end to end, and well dunged, grew large quantities of fresh vegetables for family and visitors. Also we increased our laying hens and table birds for the milk round by buying day old chicks to rear. 500 a year at monthly intervals in Spring of 100 a batch. I became adept arranging a system by which hardly a chick was lost.

Field work continued as required. I drove the odd horse or a pair through ploughing, sowing and harvesting. We attended Kingsbridge Market on Wednesdays regularly. I often drove Prudence in the market trap on other days with surplus butter, eggs and rabbits especially in winter and returned home with other supplies.

After harvest we made thatching reed from our wheat sheaves. On wet days the barn machine threshed and combed the leaf off the wheat straw to make it suitable thatching reed, which we sold to house thatchers and used to thatch our own corn and hay stacks. I liked the rick thatching, redundant now, but I still demonstrate the pleasing art at shows to-day.

Cut Hand

The first October after I left school the boss went to Tavistock Goosey Fair to buy some ewes. I having danced half the night sought an easy job. Thatching time, so I sat in the barn splitting hazel sticks to make spars with a very sharp small bill hook. Half asleep I suppose, doing what I was taught not to when cutting towards oneself the hook slipped up onto my knuckle and, I thought, cut a tendon. It was before dinner and there was a 1.30 p.m. bus from Thurlestone to catch the surgery at Kingsbridge. Mother splinted me up, I ate quickly and arrived for the doctor to confirm a cut tendon. "Have you eaten?" "Yes". "Then I can't operate until 6 p.m. You go up to the hospital and wait. The problem is the tendon ends shrink back quickly". He found and joined them, and I expected to go home, but with the hospital half empty he said "No, stay a week to 'get over the shock'". He forced a holiday on me, and with no pain I walked around chatting up the patients and nurses.

Father was shocked returning from Tavistock to be greeted by a neighbour, who, without explaining why blurted out, "Pity Hubert is in hospital!"

The first job at home to test my hand was to fence round with posts and barbed wire a huge mangold clamp. One year in October/November we carted ten acres of mangolds, double the usual. The horseman was ill, a young man and myself carted most in incessant rain. In places we sloshed through mud with carts axle deep for two or three weeks. At 40-50 cart loads the usual an acre, never less, once 70, there must have been over 200 loads, each averaging about 12 loads per day per cart. Wet through and sitting on wet sacks on the cart I developed painful haemorrhoids for a time. A cart load of mangolds is 12 cwt., with side boards on up to 1 ton.

Yes! I was dancing. My nature throughout life was to be romantic in many aspects. As children we were never allowed near a dance hall. We never heard much dance music which was thought wicked. As a boy I couldn't bear the thought of anybody wanting to cling to a flimsy clad girl and prance around a room. When 14-15 years, one summer evening with another boy and our bicycles, he said, "Let's go to South Milton, there's a dance on". His older brother danced everywhere. I hesitated but off we went. It was a beautiful evening. As we approached the hall the strains of a trombone and trumpet wafted through the air. We stopped to listen: a crooner was singing

"Goodbye Hawaii
Goodbye my isle of Paradise,
We'll meet again tomorrow, we'll meet again some day.
For my love is a love that never dies ..."

Something happened to me at that moment which changed my ideas. We watched the dancers through the door for a while. I was late home and received a telling off, but knew I wanted to dance. After I left school there happened to be lessons for ballroom dancing in our own village hall. Some time about now we bought our first wireless. Henry Hall, strict tempo and all that, to father's annoyance.

1935

On a more cheerful note, 1935 was the 25th Jubilee year of George V. With a May celebration day the village enjoyed the usual carnival in the morning, sports and tea in the afternoon and a barn dance in the evening. We entered the carnival with Prudence in the market trap rigged up with us as gipsies, my oldest sister's idea. It was a rush to finish the milk round, and so realistic were we that going back through the village to the starting point we were not recognised. We heard, "Oh! Look at these old gipsies coming! We don't want them here today!" We took first prize which resulted in us leading the parade.

In the afternoon I excelled at the sports taking many prizes. I left school mentally and physically alert, and found little opposition locally, except that I was surprised in the high jump by a neighbouring farmer twice my age. In fact he was captain of the football team that won the cup in 1927. He out jumped me in '35. Also there was no team to challenge the heavy local pub tug-of-war team, so I selected hurriedly a scratch team of youngsters on the field and we pulled them pretty comfortably and won, much to everyone's surprise. Which proved what father and myself already knew, that there is no work in alcohol, only the thought that there is.

Exhausted we returned home to milk the cows, then I lay on the bed to recover before returning to the revelry of the dance.

Change

Our way of life was changing. Firstly from the accumulator operated portable wireless set (we had no mains electricity): we could tune in to every kind of music, world news as it happened, talks and dramas from a variety of cultures sensationally brought into our living room. For instance father became enamoured with Gracie Fields singing, a fantastic voice. I had heard him sing little but hymns. Now we caught him humming dance tunes, 'Little old lady dressed in blue' and 'Twas on the Isle of Capri that I found her'. His eight o'clock bed time often became nine if he wished to hear the news, eating his bread and milk as he listened. He even stayed up later if Len Harvey the heavyweight Cornish boxer was fighting.

Secondly from silent films to the escapism of the fantastic American high life on the talking celluloid. In its heyday in the 30s with such wondrous films like Ginger Rogers and Fred Astaire's, and Busby Berkeley's marvels. We boys cycled to Kingsbridge often on Saturday nights. Occasionally the family would hire a taxi to the cinema and back.

Thirdly it had to come, there were arrangements for a car to be bought from a local garage. At seventeen years I was old enough to drive. Father had much soul searching, but the deal didn't come off, much to the annoyance of the garage owner. It happened that a farmer friend about to buy new offered us his old Clyno in running order for £10. I was expected to drive it but first was not sure that I wanted to take on the responsibility of a possible killing machine, as cars were already known.

It was now the first year of the driving test. I failed first time on a question from the introduction to the code book, which I had never bothered to read. The second time I drove worse but passed. Later I found that I need not have been tested, as a licence was acquired for me in 1935 before tests started. I still have it.

These three changes as much as anything began the break up of our subculture of two thousand years or more. Especially the motor car. A saloon car was faster, more comfortable and cosier than horse transport. Therefore one could travel farther afield and back in the same time, all in the warmth. It was desirable and catching so we grew softer in the new luxury.

Young Farmers Club

In 1934 Kingsbridge Young Farmers Club was formed. We were asked to be founder members, but my father wasn't too sure that it was right for us. I feel now that there were many things he did not like if they took us beyond his control. But he was persuaded and my third sister and self joined the following year, both of us under 21 years, the limit. One of the twins joined later.

Y.F.C. activities were monthly meetings, lectures, practical teaching classes ending with competitions, and socially our dances were very popular. But the main activity was rearing calves to 12 months old when an annual show judged for prize winners in two or three classes. The young calves were firstly bought for us by our parent Committee, then we drew numbers for our allotted calf. I was very lucky and for three years drew a good calf, each won a 1st prize and the third the overall championship. My sisters were not so lucky, each one won a second prize I believe. Of course we molly-coddled them, especially the girls, but the feeding was all important, 'nine tenths of the pedigree goes in at the mouth'. Again father's expertise was crucial, he understood the correct rations in balanced diet, not overdosing with the proprietary calf foods on offer. So we learned.

The second year the club tried pigs, my sisters didn't but I drew one of the allotted young gilts, reared and farrowed it with eight piglets in time for the annual show. Knowing nothing of showing pigs I scrubbed the gilt with shampoo the night before and bedded her in clean straw. In the morning I wanted her to look glowing in health and hit on an idea and brushed her over with liquid paraffin. She was of saddle back breed and her black coat shone like patent shoes. Many asked me how I achieved it. She was outstanding and won first prize. I never revealed how. The next year our club bought piglets with a chest infection, a disaster, most died of pneumonia including mine.

One aim of Y.F.C. was that members should socialise and we visited each other's farms. The boys vied with each other in strength contests. We believed we were men when able to throw a bullock, by holding a horn with one hand and a finger and thumb in its nostrils with the other: then turn its head up one side and one shoulder would drop towards the ground. When fully on its side keep its head down by sitting on it. The bullock couldn't rise, was yours.

Have car, will travel

We did travel, especially me the only driver, later two sisters and father drove. Useful for Y.F.C. events, markets, farm sales, visiting relatives and friends, occasional afternoon off. These were big changes.

Before, I often cycled and was invited to join Kingsbridge soccer and cricket clubs. For away matches I went without dinner and cycled to be on Kingsbridge quay for the bus at 1.30 p.m. I didn't drink or smoke for fitness sake. Returning, the other men visited pubs and they liked to arrive at Kingsbridge by 9.50 for a last drink. I have to cycle 5 miles home. One night arriving home at 10.30 I found father again sat up bathing his feet. I never knew why. He didn't look up, but said, "Your five cows aren't milked, the fat bullocks aren't fed, nor the yearlings in the shed". I turned out and did it without a word, but that ended the soccer until I captained our village team set up sometime in the war. At hay harvest time I pleaded with father to allow me a cricket match. Reluctantly he agreed. After the match some boys learned there was a dance in a nearby village hall. I cycled home at 1 a.m. That ended cricket.

It happened the D.C.C. Agricultural classes were to be repeated at Kingsbridge Grammar School. I joined them one night a week by car. In 1937 came George VI's coronation, after Duke of Windsor, Mrs. Simpson and all that. At the village celebration 3 other boys and self on Duke as Uncle Tom Cobley and all, won, again, 1st prize and led the carnival procession. I didn't fare so well in sports as '35, a better athlete had come to live in the village.

In the evening the car allowed us to visit the firework display at Kingsbridge. I met a pretty golden haired girl and fell head over heels on sight. A sudden attack of love-sickness and don't tell me that is not a real illness. I did not know how to cope with it or how to treat a girl. Should she read this now I hope she will forgive me. After the K.G.S. classes weekly we went to the cinema and I drove her home. For a time we danced together quite a lot. Sadly it caused friction at home because the car was away so often. My mileage was being checked. After all it was father's car.

At the end of the Agricultural Course I gained a 2nd Class certificate. Possibly I should have done better, but my mind was elsewhere.

1938

With extra cattle reared we were able to put some away to summer grazing enabling more cropping or hay to be cut at home. Lipton was offering two fields of which of course father knew the worth. We walked 10-12 young cattle the 10 miles through Kingsbridge and sister fetched us by car. It was the first time I saw Lipton farmhouse, not remembering it when young . When the grazing finished enterprisingly father looked over a 150 acre derelict farm he knew of. It was full of rough grazing. The owner agreed for us to winter our cattle running over most of it. He paid a retired man he knew to see them once a day, and we borrowed a bull to put with them. They returned to Lipton to graze another summer and back again to the rough grazing for another winter. Finally we brought home 26-28 as I remember, a herd that would start anyone farming. Not my luck however so to do peacefully, Hitler was ranting and raging.

Conclusion.

The limit for this publication has been reached and at the end of my school years I had made up my mind to farm in our beloved valley. All attempts to lure me away had failed. A challenging career, as farming is, lay ahead. To work with my father and our staff at livestock and cropping skills of which I had the basic knowledge and could only improve. The business side was more tricky and difficult.

There were five years after school through which we carried on our traditional mixed farming, but changes were creeping in, i.e. wireless (radio) and a motor car. These were revolutionary. Even so, life was not easy, and working for your own father may not always be wise.

The great change for everybody came in 1939 when that summer produced a feeling of unreality and disbelief. It wasn't happening to us: the start of the Second Great War. Day by day new war decrees were announced and advancing technology eroded our stable way of farming for another mechanised one, ever advancing to the doom of working horses that gradually disappeared. But these years are another story, hopefully to follow this one in due course.